Staying the Course

Staying

the

Course

Supporting the Church's Position on Homosexuality

Edited by

Maxie D. Dunnam
and
H. Newton Malony

Abingdon Press
NASHVILLE

STAYING THE COURSE
SUPPORTING THE CHURCH'S POSITION ON HOMOSEXUALITY

Library of Congress Cataloging-in-Publication Data

Staying the course : supporting the church's position on homosexuality
/ edited by Maxie D. Dunnam and H. Newton Malony.
 p. cm.
Includes bibliographical references.
 ISBN 0-687-04534-7 (pbk. : alk. paper)
 1. Homosexuality—Religious aspects—United Methodist Church (U.S.)
2. United Methodist Church (U.S.)—Doctrines. I. Dunnam, Maxie D. II.
Malony, H. Newton.

BX8349.H66 S73 2002
261.8'35766'08827—dc21

 2002152777

03 04 05 06 07 08 09 10 11 12—10 9 8 7 6 5 4 3 2 1

MANUFACTURED IN THE UNITED STATES OF AMERICA

Contents

Foreword

David Brooks, writing an article entitled, "One Nation, Slightly Divisible,"[1] called attention to the political, cultural, and social contrast in the United States made evident by the 2000 presidential race. Brooks focused on the electoral map used by television, on which big blocks of red (denoting states that went to President Bush) dominated the heartland of America, and ribbons of blue (denoting states for Vice President Gore) appeared along the coasts. Brooks asked the basic question, "Do our differences effectively split us into two nations, or are there just cracks in a still-united whole?"

Red America, according to Brooks, is the land of Wal-Mart, NASCAR, country music, barbecue restaurants and Cracker Barrel, pickup trucks and bass boats, small colleges and large land grant universities (with big budgets for college football), and QVC. Blue America is a land of elite boutiques, NPR, Thai restaurants, Volvos and Audis, Ivy League schools or Stanford, and soccer or sailing.

Obviously Brooks exaggerates in order to make his point. He even eventually concludes that the values that unite us as a nation transcend the regional divisions that make us such a curious people. However, his fundamental question has haunted me because I believe it is a key question, not only for our nation, but also for our beloved United Methodist Church. Do our differences effectively split us into two or more churches, or are our differences simply cracks in the still-united whole?

Even a casual observer to our recent General Conference, or for that matter, to a Council of Bishops meeting, could not fail to recognize the theological, social, cultural, and regional differences in our Church. Sometimes we also begin to look like the "Red and Blue America" that Brooks described. Regional voting is reflective of the fact that we live in very different types of communities, and our life experiences are not as similar as might have been the case in previous generations. United Methodism continues to grow, albeit slightly, in the heartland of America. The Southeastern and South Central Jurisdictions continue to emerge as stronger centers of our denomination's life. We continue to lose membership in the Northeast and the West, which characteristically have tended to be more theologically liberal. This evolving geographical reality within our Church has, by itself, created some strain and stress in our connection. And, of course, our diversity extends far beyond the borders of the United States of America. The growing influence of our sisters and brothers in the Central Conferences has challenged all of us to think outside an American context. In fact, the growing multicultural and multinational nature of United Methodism may turn out to be one of our saving graces, saving us from our American addictions to amusement, affluence, and power.

One of the most visible manifestations of our divisions has been the issue of homosexuality. This issue has been the "lightning rod" on our Church's agenda. The controversy crescendos every four years at General Conference, resulting in petitions, impassioned speeches, demonstrations, intimidations, and arrests. During these thirty years of debate, our Church has continued to maintain a biblically and classically orthodox position on the subject of homosexuality. We have not affirmed homosexual lifestyles as consistent with the holiness of life expressed in Scripture. We have by majorities of 75 to 80 percent chosen to maintain the orthodox Christian stance, which has dominated Christian understanding for two thousand years. We have affirmed that homosexual persons are welcomed in our churches, where we all together examine our lifestyles, thoughts, and motives by the light of the gospel of Jesus Christ. The United Methodist Church's position is compassionate yet firm.

This book offers a variety of significant essays, which I hope will be helpful to us as we continue in Christian conversation on this frustrating and painful subject. Some of us may have grown weary of the conversation, but let us persevere in the hope that the Lord can lead us in our discernments and loving responses to one another. These essays are thoughtful and respectful. They represent an honest attempt to be clear about our beliefs and our feelings, and I hope you will prayerfully consider each of them.

On a pastoral note, as a Bishop in the Church, I yearn for a time in the future when we can move this issue off the front burner of the denomination and proceed to use our best energies to focus on our primary evangelistic task and to confront what I believe to be the more important social issues of our day—world poverty and its effects on children, violence, pornography, racism, drug and substance abuse, healthcare, and the emerging ethical questions made relevant by the twenty-first-century biotechnology.

Bishop G. Lindsey Davis

Preface

A colleague recently asked, "Who would have thought that homosexuality would have become the defining issue for the church at the beginning of the twenty-first century?" No one we know would have predicted the prominence questions about homosexuality have assumed in this postmodern atmosphere. Feelings are intense; and the dialogue, unfortunately, has deteriorated into name-calling. As among those who have taken a conservative point of view, it pains us deeply to have those on the other side label our opinions as "homophobic," "heterosexist," or "biblically literalistic." We firmly deny the validity of any of these labels and feel the discussion deserves more thoughtful and reasonable debate than such appellations evoke. We consider these labels as pejorative and offensive as labels such as "heterophobic," "homosexist," or "biblical revisionist" might seem to others. It is unfortunate that political correctness now dominates the discussion, and those who affirm the traditional approach to these matters are considered to be prejudiced, unjust, and autocratic.

We offer the essays in this volume as a counter to such stereotypes. We fully affirm the statements about sexuality embedded in *The Book of Discipline* of The United Methodist Church and are convinced that their formulation was inspired by the Holy Spirit. We believe that the insights they reflect are firmly grounded in biblical, theological, ethical, and scientific understandings. Furthermore, we are convinced that these disciplinary affirmations are consonant with the heritage of the church universal and, more particularly, with the tradition of the Wesleyan movement. Our forefather, John Wesley, was convinced that the role of the church was to redeem fallen creation, not to conform to changing customs—as others would seem to recommend.

Included in this compilation are respected authors from some of the nation's major seminaries as well as well-informed experts from the pastoral and counseling worlds. We believe their ideas and opinions are worthy of serious consideration in the current dialogue. We recognize that the issues surrounding sexuality in general and homosexuality in particular have risen to great prominence in annual, jurisdictional, and general conference deliberations over the past decade. While statements emanating from a few of these meetings have taken exception to some of the *Discipline*'s statements, the convictions of the General Conference have been reaffirmed by increasing majority votes. We prayerfully applaud the General Conference for these actions and offer this volume as a principled foundation for their actions. Although we see no need for a win-lose encounter over these issues, we are convinced that The United Methodist Church needs to be firm in its convictions at the same time that it continues to welcome every person into a fellowship of grace, forgiveness, and power.

We assume the motivations of those who see these matters from a different perspective are genuine, loving, and Christian. We trust that they perceive us in the same light. However, lest our intentions be misunderstood, we feel it necessary to clarify our approach a bit. We do not condone prejudice, discrimination, or violence, although we feel it is appropriate to assert ourselves when we feel demands are for *privileges* more than *rights*. We welcome all persons into the fellowship of the church but see no need to place homosexuals into some special category separate from the rest of us to whom Christ offers forgiveness, reconciliation, and transformation. We resist any commandeering of words like "inclusiveness" and "welcoming" by those who take a different point of view. We strongly support *including* homosexuals among those whose lives can be transformed, and we *welcome* homosexuals into the life of the church where we, like they, have the opportunity to live by the forgiving grace of God.

Maxie D. Dunnam and H. Newton Malony
Trinity Season
2002

PART I: THE CHURCH

CHAPTER 1

The Church's Teaching on Sexuality

A Defense of The United Methodist Church's *Discipline* on Homosexuality

William J. Abraham

Introduction

*T*he moral and theological propriety of homosexual practice has now been on the agenda of The United Methodist Church for a generation. Two things are immediately clear. First, it is highly unlikely that there will be any dramatic change in the Church's stance in the foreseeable future. The Church has spoken again and again over the last thirty years, and predictions or promises of imminent change have failed to be realized. Second, it is obvious to the serious observer that much more is at stake than the morality of same-sex intimacy. It is surely clear that epistemological and ecclesiological issues are crucial in the discussion.[1] Given the contested nature of these matters, it is not surprising that no one to date has offered a robust defense of our Church's position.[2] In this paper I intend to make good on this deficiency.[3]

Specifically, I would like to do five things. First, I want to review the position of the United Methodist *Book of Discipline* on the topic of homosexuality. Second, I want to indicate where I think there is significant agreement across the current positions that have been adopted. Third, I want to note where the crucial differences lie. Fourth, in and through these efforts I want to indicate why I think *The Book of Discipline* is essentially correct, responding where appropriate to various objections and explaining why the commitment to it is so tenacious and urgent. Fifth and finally, I want to show that the position of *The Book of Discipline* fits neatly with at least one crucial element in any robust ecclesiology that can claim to be United Methodist in orientation.

The Position of *The Book of Discipline*

The core teaching of The United Methodist Church on homosexuality is relatively simple and straightforward:

> Homosexual persons no less than heterosexual persons are individuals of sacred worth. All persons need the ministry and guidance of the Church in their struggles for human fulfillment, as well as the spiritual and emotional care of a fellowship that enables reconciling relationships with God, others, and with self. Although we do not condone the practice of homosexuality and consider this practice incompatible with Christian teaching, we affirm that God's grace is available to all. We commit ourselves to be in ministry for and with all persons.[4]

Whatever our judgment on the merits of this paragraph, we can surely agree that this is a well-crafted and judicious statement. Generally speaking, I am not usually enamored with the rhetoric of ecclesiastical pronouncements, for they tend to be written in what the English philosopher, Basil Mitchell, once called "trade union English." However, this statement from *The Book of Discipline* is as good as one can get outside English Anglicanism, the leader in felicitous religious prose of this kind.

Four distinct elements are crucial to this paragraph. First, there is a distinction between persons and their sexual behavior, between persons and their actions. This is not a redeployment of the old distinction between the sinner and the sin. The move here is correctly positive in its anthropological content, insisting that all persons are of sacred worth. It begins with persons before they are sinners, so to speak. Even then, this language is perhaps too thin and emaciated. What we really want to say is that all persons are made in the

16

image and likeness of God and all persons have been redeemed at an incredible price by the precious blood of Christ. This is the basis of their sacred worth, and it is one of the reasons we must distinguish between person and act. Given the distinction between person and act, our Church insists that it is possible to be fully committed to the welfare of the person even though one disagrees with the moral character of her or his behavior.

Second, it is claimed that the *practice* of homosexuality is incompatible with Christian teaching. This claim is at once both substantive and modest. It is substantive where it needs to be, that is, in saying cleanly what is at stake on the first-order moral question at issue. Hence, it is substantive in that it draws a line in the sand and says that homosexual practices lie outside the boundary of acceptable Christian teaching. It is equally modest where it needs to be, that is, in second-order questions about justification and warrant. This is a reticent claim, for it leaves a host of questions unanswered about the identity and warrants for Christian teaching. The teaching of the Church also rightly does not tackle the complex matter of pastoral care, surely something that cannot be micromanaged with appropriate sophistication in any ecclesiastical pronouncement. Not surprisingly these lacunae create ample space for discussion and debate.

Third, it is affirmed that God's grace is available to all. Again, this is modest, but we can surely assume that what is at stake here is the whole panoply of grace, that is, prevenient, justifying, and sanctifying grace. Recovering this way of thinking and speaking is one of the jewels of the last generation's work in Wesley studies and on splendid display here, even if it remains tacit.

Fourth, there is a commitment to be in ministry for and with all persons. Our Church is resolute in its inclusivity at this point. We covenant to be engaged in a comprehensive ministry for and with everybody.

These four distinct elements in the church's teaching are intimately related to a wider network of conviction. In *The Book of Discipline,* they are, on the one hand, foregrounded by claims about the sanctity of marriage, the possibility of divorce, the integrity of single persons, the common humanity of male and female, the recognition of sexuality as a good gift from God, the need for careful and extensive study of sexuality, the place of marriage in sexual intimacy, the rejection of all forms of sexual abuse, the embrace of human and civil rights for all, and the importance of sex education. On the other hand, these claims about homosexuality are followed by sensitive recommendations about family violence, sexual harassment, abortion, and adoption.

Significant Areas of Agreement

In the current climate, it is very tempting to cut to the chase and identify the sharp differences that have emerged in evaluation of this material. Before doing so, we should relax and make note of areas of agreement. There is clearly enormous overlap between the various positions that are advocated. Here I shall highlight only three.

We all agree that sex is a good gift from God that finds its proper place within lasting covenant relations. I take it that such a view undergirds the move to develop rites for same-sex unions or marriages. Here we differ quite radically from our popular Western culture, in which sex is essentially seen as a good indoor sport. In the culture of the popular chat shows, we know what the basic message about sex is: Anything goes so long as the participants agree (the principle of consent) and no one gets hurt (the principle of utility). Over against this, we can agree that sex is intrinsically connected to covenant and commitment.

Second, we agree that the matter of sexual practices, generally, and homosexual practices, particularly, cannot be abstracted from sophisticated doctrines of creation and redemption. We are not secularists on these matters. Our views on sexuality are embedded in complex visions of the human situation and its redemption through Jesus Christ. Hence, we desire to speak and think as Christians informed by an appropriate theological assessment of our relationship with God.

Third, we agree that as United Methodists we are committed to consulting Scripture on the issues at stake. We need not at this stage agree to that great Methodist icon in epistemology, the Quadrilateral.[5] Nor need we agree in detail on the content or application of pertinent empirical information, whether formal or anecdotal. Yet we do agree that as United Methodists we are bound to consult the Scriptures of the church and take them with the utmost seriousness.[6]

Getting Below the Surface of Our Differences

Once we go beyond these generalities, deep differences begin to surface. In pursuing these differences, it is important to get beyond initial impressions and explore why the differences are significant. This is easily missed in the current climate. The temptation is to focus on the material content of the disagreements and ignore the status of the disagreements. As a result, the consequences of the potential division of the Church are ignored or treated as merely emotional or political. Given this disposition, it is not surprising that current church leaders have enormous difficulty facing up to the situation in the church at large. This, at least, has been my experience in dialogues both formal and informal. Efforts merely to get clear on what is before us are treated with either incomprehension or hostility simply because we cannot get below the surface.

Equally, there is a widespread tendency to focus merely on what our own personal commitments are on the various issues and to ignore completely the corporate, or canonical, commitments of The United Methodist Church on the issues.[7] No doubt this is in part a by-product of Enlightenment individualism, but even those who can readily and aggressively identify the corporate dimensions of moral issues fail to reckon with the corporate or canonical or institutional commitments of the Church as a whole.

As to our differences, it is now pretty common knowledge where they lie, so I can mention them summarily. First, we differ in the morality of homosexual practice. Some consider all homosexual practice as contrary to the will of God and morally unacceptable. Others believe that homosexual practice should be held to the same standards as heterosexual practice, and that same-sex unions or marriages should be permitted. Second, we differ in our sociological expectations. Some believe that it will be possible to arrive at an acceptable form of marriage for homosexuals, one that will be generally adopted by homosexuals within the Church, if not within the culture. Others, drawing attention to the rising voice of bisexual persons, seriously doubt this. Third, we differ in what are and are not acceptable boundaries within the life of the Church. Compatibilists hold that we can contain the current differences on homosexual practice within the one denomination. Incompatibilists do not. This is essentially a difference in ecclesiology. Finally, we differ on what warrants to deploy in arguments related to morality and ecclesiology. Put grandly, we differ in the epistemology of theology. Let me pursue this fourth difference in some detail; for contrary to first impressions, this matter is very important to understanding our ecclesiology.[8]

In Search of a Methodological Triumph

At a popular level the differences about homosexuality are very quickly cast in terms of a debate about Scripture.[9] Those who are more conservative typically marshal a series of exegetical arguments from various texts in, say, Genesis, Leviticus, and Paul. These arguments are backed up in various ways with appeals to the tradition of the church, scientific data about sexual identity, general proposals about the promise of grace in the gospel, and contemporary experiences of transformation. Those who are more liberal in turn seek to take the sting out of the various scriptural texts by arguing that they do not bear the meaning attributed to them, or by proposing that crucial parts of Scripture, notably the Gospels, do not speak to the issue. Positively, they appeal to general principles of Scripture embodied in such themes as inclusivity, the universal working of grace, liberation, justice, or compassion.

In much of this debate, protagonists on both sides seek to resolve the debate by appealing to some sort of decisive methodological principle that will bring everybody to heel. Clearly, given the Protestant orientation of United Methodism, one of the favorite methodological moves is to deploy some sort of appeal to *sola scriptura*. This is often the rallying cry of conservatives. Not surprisingly this move has not succeeded in resolving the matter; we should not be surprised at this outcome, as I shall show in a moment.[10] On the liberal side, the decisive methodological principle takes a variety of forms: an appeal to scientific data on the etiology of gender identity or an appeal to the cultural construction of gender concepts or an appeal to a simple pastoral mandate to minister to all people or a moral appeal to eliminate the last great vestige of discrimination in North American culture or a liturgical appeal of baptism. This list grows from time to time, but the main items are now relatively clear and exhaustive.

It would be easy to grow intellectually cynical in listening to the debate: It is as if folk have already decided the issue and then cast around for any warrant that will carry the day. Thus, liberals readily point out that conservatives do not follow scriptural teaching on divorce or women's ordination, suggesting that they are really driven by contemporary bourgeois morality rather than by Scripture. Conservatives, in turn, charge that liberals merely pay lip service to Scripture and are really caving in to political correctness or to the conventions of a post-Christian culture after the sexual revolution of the 1960s.

It would be nice to resolve all this by appeal to the Quadrilateral of Scripture, tradition, reason, and experience. This was essentially the stance of the late Albert Outler. In a photocopy of a letter in my personal possession, Outler suggests that the Quadrilateral convincingly supports the official position of the Church.[11] Hence, conservatives can legitimately claim the backing of Outler for their position. I can only wave a hand at this topic at this point, but suffice it to say here that the Quadrilateral fails to carry the day for obvious reasons. First, it fails because liberals have equally appealed to the Quadrilateral to support their case. Indeed, the Quadrilateral is often seen as crucial to the more liberal case. Second, the appeal to the Quadrilateral will only carry weight for those who continue to support it as crucial to our understanding of Wesley, for those who think that it is essential to United Methodist identity, and for those who hold that it is still a viable epistemological project for today. Insofar as any or all of these claims are undermined, then the Quadrilateral will cease to be of any substantive value in resolving the current disputes. It cannot function as a methodological holy grail.

A Tempting Conclusion

In these circumstances it is tempting to draw the following conclusion. Having explored the matter for a generation, high up and low down, United Methodists cannot agree on the content of their position on homosexual practice, on their sociological expectation, on their ecclesiology, or on the warrants for their position. The sensible and fair thing to do in these circumstances is to live and let live. Should we not acknowledge the diversity and permit a variety of opinion and practice? Effectively this was the position of the 1992 report to General Conference.[12] With appropriate

21

accommodation and enrichment it is essentially the position of many who are working to revise *The Book of Discipline*. All they want, they say, is the freedom to follow through on their convictions. Moreover, opposition to this sensible proposal is seen as intellectually odd, politically motivated, and morally mean. Opposition is essentially intolerant, whereas the state of debate warrants inclusivity, diversity, and tolerance.

Recasting the Categories of the Debate

Prima facie I grant immediately the plausibility of this conclusion. Like many initial and sensible conclusions, however, it will not stand up to scrutiny. In overturning it I want in what follows to get at the underlying warrant for the position of *The Book of Discipline*. I shall also provide an alternative reading for the tenacity of those who are committed to that position. In pursuing this line of argument, perceptive observers will note not only that I want to recast the terms of the debate, moving beyond the sterile terms in which it is often stated, but also that I want to make an appeal to the canonical commitments of our Church.

What is at stake in the debate, as we noted earlier, is not just what happens in the bedroom. but a whole vision of human existence under God. What we need to note is that although this vision is in a real sense rooted in Scripture, it is not merely read off Scripture or deductively proved from Scripture. In a certain sense, like the great doctrines of the Trinity and the incarnation, this vision is not worked out apart from Scripture, yet it is above and beyond Scripture.[13]

Consider the crucial claim that we should distinguish between persons and their acts. Let's call this the person/act principle. This principle is not simply some sort of biblical axiom. There are, in fact, all sorts of compelling arguments in favor of it. One might argue, for example, that this principle is easily established by reflection on one's own moral actions. We can and do distinguish between the persons we are and the actions we perform.[14] Thus, in the Irish political situation, one can be committed to the welfare of terrorists by insisting on respect for their rights, and at the same time still reject the evil they do. One does not need to appeal to Scripture to establish this. Moreover, this is so even though the per-

22

son/act principle can easily be derived in various ways from Scripture, for instance from the Pauline claims that while we were yet sinners, Christ died for us, or from the Johannine account of our Lord's treatment of the woman caught in adultery. What matters is that this axiom is not necessarily held because one is committed to Scripture.[15]

What is said here about the distinction between persons and their actions could be extended to the complex mass of claims in *The Book of Discipline,* in which the comments about homosexual practice are embedded. The upshot of this observation is that *sola scriptura* is more often than not a red herring in the debate. As a slogan, *sola scriptura* has been invaluable in exhorting us to read and preach Scripture, as it did in Pietism; and it has enabled us to recover Scripture when buried under mountains of tradition, as it did at the Reformation. However, the appeal to Scripture in the debate about homosexual practice has also led to a trivializing of the debate. Let me explain why this is the case.

Essentially, the issue has been turned into a quotation contest centered narrowly on a handful of texts, in which everything has been reduced to the pitting of one interpretation against another. As soon as Scripture is brought in, the cry goes up, "But this is just your interpretation of the text, and I have my expert professional at my sleeve to trump any expert you have at yours." So conservatives appeal to Professor Richard Hays, and liberals appeal to Professor Victor Furnish. After we are exhausted at this level, then the debate moves to the integration of scriptural material into data gathered from science and experience, and again we are back in an Irish bog, in which one interpretation can always look as good as another. We sink into a sea of opinion and interpretation that loses the specificity of the claims at issue and that cannot cope with the passion and tenacity with which they are held and advanced.[16]

Switching from Scripture to Revelation

We need at this point to think again, and we can begin with the appeal to Scripture. The deep insight in the appeal to Scripture lies elsewhere than in a simple application of some ancient text. The enduring strength of drawing on Scripture in the Christian church is that it is essentially an appeal to special revelation. In insisting on the cruciality of Scripture, what folk are groping for is this: We only partially know who we are, what our nature is, and how we are to live, by appeal to reason and experience. Reason and experience, though important and even indispensable, are insufficient and inadequate. We depend substantially and nontrivially on divine revelation. So what conservatives are really getting at is that it is through divine revelation that we know our true nature as God intended it to be.

In these circumstances, it is not enough to announce a new anthropological insight derived from modern studies of sexuality. What we believe or do not believe about divine revelation in part determines how we conceive of our nature. There is no necessary cozy correlation between the content of revelation and what we derive from science and experience.[17] Our ordinary deliberations about human nature are shot through with mystery, distortion, half-truth, and partial insight. Much of this can be gathered up and transfigured by divine revelation, but our ordinary deliberations are not at all adequate in themselves. In an appropriate way God has revealed himself and his ways to us. In redemption and salvation we are invited to live a life befitting such revelation.

Crossing the Threshold of Divine Revelation

Casting the issue in terms of revelation completely alters the terms of the debate in several ways.

First, it is hopelessly inadequate to reduce the issue to the pitting of one scriptural interpretation against another. Revelation, unlike Scripture, is a threshold concept. It is like crossing through a doorway into a whole new world that is not available to us until we get inside it and begin to explore it for ourselves. To be sure, one has to identify a revelation. To be sure, one has to interpret a revelation. To be sure, one has to think through the application of divine revelation in new cultural or intellectual situations. All these require the full mustering of all our cognitive capacities. However, once one comes to see something as revelation, then one has crossed over into a world in which he or she has to treat the revelation as knowledge. One has to obey it, to hold tenaciously and even passionately to it, and in some instances to be prepared to die for it.

It is very easy to miss this point by retorting that when it comes to revelation the whole debate about the interpretation of revelation breaks out again. As I have mentioned, of course, one has to interpret a revelation. However, there is all the difference in the world in what is at stake once the issue is cast in terms of revelation. One is no longer simply wrestling with a book or a set of texts. One is wrestling with the will of God. Sooner or later, whatever the complexity of interpretation, one has to fish or cut bait. Either there is or there is not a revelation. Either one has or has not gotten hold of it. Once these issues are decided, one has crossed the threshold; and the call to treat the putative revelation as knowledge, to obey it, to be tenacious in holding to it, and to die for it kicks in immediately. We are no longer living in the cozy, comfortable middle-class world of the academy. We are dealing with the Word of God.[18]

Second, the crucial texts are no longer confined to the standard list of texts in the Old or New Testament that focus on word studies and on this or that prohibition. These have their place in the debate on sexuality. Indeed, maintaining a sophisticated vision of all life under God appears across the span of the Old and New Testaments is one of the tasks of moral theology. However, the really crucial texts become those that represent the teaching of our Lord on marriage. Once one works with divine revelation, our Lord's teaching cannot be simply added in as one more item in a list of texts; it has to come front and center in our deliberations. In this instance one has to come to terms with his appeal to the creation narrative in Genesis and to the divine intention for marriage as a specific divine calling in which male and female are joined in lifelong commitment.[19] Despite disclaimers to the contrary, this text speaks very directly to the matter of same-sex unions.[20] To be sure, in our current situation, the teaching of our Lord amounts to a hard saying; but this is the case with much of his teaching, so we are on thoroughly familiar territory.[21]

To be sure, we can once again begin the reductionistic game of pitting one interpretation against another. Once we do, revelation is lost in a sea of human opinion, so that the whole idea of something made appropriately clear by God is buried under a mountain of rubble. Modern historical study, as represented by the Jesus Seminar, only deepens the layers one can assemble.[22] However, when cast in terms of revelation, the matter takes on entirely different features. Sooner or later one must come to terms with what is the teaching, not just of some ancient text, but the teaching of our Lord and Savior Jesus Christ. Put this in place, and we are back over the threshold already mentioned above. However much we may hesitate, study, reflect, debate, and discuss, there comes a point when we must either fish or cut bait. Either we do or we do not cross the threshold of divine revelation. We are no longer dealing merely with human judgment and opinion, even though we use human judgment and opinion to get to that point where we do or do not cross over.[23]

Third, the interpretation and reception of revelation are never merely a human exercise. One receives and hears divine revelation through the work of the Holy Spirit. This takes us way beyond mere exegesis and inference, indispensable as these are. Revelation is received through prayer, fasting, and the pursuit of virtue. Moreover, one listens to revelation not just in the company of scholars, but more important in the company of the saints and martyrs. In recent United Methodist theology this has been cast in terms of listening to tradition. However, this is much too weak and secular a notion. It does not begin to do justice to the spiritual sensitivity and personal transformation that is at stake. It is more apt to say that we listen to divine revelation in the company of the saints in the Holy Spirit.

A Word on Divorce

Much of the Church's appropriation of our Lord's teaching on divorce has missed this subtle practice of listening with the saints in the Holy Spirit. The standard procedure in the West has been either to take a hard line in the name of revelation, as happens in Roman Catholicism, or to ignore it and look the other way in the name of compassion and grace, as happens in mainline Protestantism. Knowing the position of *The Book of Discipline* on divorce and the practice of conservatives, liberals within United Methodism have been quick to charge conservatives with self-serving inconsistency. The matter is more complex, however, as is clear from the alternative reception of the relevant material within the Eastern Orthodox tradition. The proposal is that tradition runs like this: Marriage is God's design; within the calling of marriage, male and female are to be joined together in lifelong commitment. However, for many reasons marriages do break down. In compassion, the Church understands this and both permits and performs marriage after divorce. However, this is done in such a way as to acknowledge the intention of God in marriage; hence, second or third marriages are prefaced with a fitting form of repentance for past failure. In United Methodism, we have rightly gone the way of the Eastern Orthodox tradition without fully acknowledging its sensitivity and strength and without capturing liturgically the complexity of our situation before God. Hence, *The Book of Discipline* has gotten the matter essentially if not comprehensively right on both homosexual practice and divorce. The popular attempt to claim some kind of inconsistency within *The Book of Discipline* fails completely to reckon with the subtlety of the issues at hand.

A Word on Women's Ordination

Another standard charge made is that if one supports the position of *The Book of Discipline* on homosexual practice, one should also be opposed to the ordination of women. For liberals interested in skillful polemic and the quick kill, this is a godsend. However, as with divorce, we have moved much too fast, and I want to use this issue to segue into a matter of the profoundest importance in the current debate.

The claim that conservatives who support the teaching of *The Book of Discipline* on homosexuality should somehow be opposed to women's ordination is built on two assumptions. First, there is the assumption that conservatives are committed to a naïve view of *sola scriptura;* and, second, there is the assumption that Scripture provides some sort of blueprint for ministry in the church. As I have already mentioned, the appeal to Scripture is crucially an appeal to divine revelation. This is the deep insight buried in the conservative disposition to appeal to Scripture. Moreover, it is foolish in the extreme to argue that an appeal either to Scripture or to divine revelation commits one to the view that we have a blueprint for ministry in the Church. The Reformation debates about the warrants for ecclesiological practices make this patently clear. The judicious Richard Hooker effectively won the day against the Presbyterians and the Independents, and Wesley and the whole

Methodist family of churches stand in the succession of Hooker on this issue. This tradition is clear in insisting that since there is no blueprint on ministry in Scripture, no blueprint on the gender of those ordained can be derived from Scripture. Hence, one can be totally committed to our Lord's teaching on marriage without at all being committed to an exclusively male ministry of the ordained. To put these in the same boat—the nature of marriage and the internal organization of the Church—is to make an obvious and elementary blunder. How all this is to be argued in detail cannot be worked out here, of course; but enough has been said to undercut the standard claim that one cannot be committed to the position of *The Book of Discipline* on homosexual practice and also be committed to women's ordination.[24]

The Place of Revelation in the Canonical Commitments of The United Methodist Church

Consider now a point that is in the neighborhood. What I am deploying here is broadly if not precisely the canonical position of The United Methodist Church on its warrants for any theological proposal.[25] Despite popular mythology to the contrary, The United Methodist Church is committed neither to a doctrine of *sola scriptura* nor to the Quadrilateral. As its Articles of Religion and Confession of Faith in the *Discipline* make clear, our Church sees Scripture primarily in soteriological categories. Moreover, our Church canonically proposes that divine revelation be its fundamental epistemic category in matters of theological warrant, and it eschews any claim that revelation or Scripture provide a blueprint for its structures and forms of ministry.[26] Hence, if we are to move beyond merely arguing our case in standard Enlightenment, and now postmodern, fashion, that is, in terms of our own private and personal categories, we need to work through both the clarity and the complexity of divine revelation.

Tenacity and Urgency

There is yet one more observation in the neighborhood that dovetails with these considerations. Once one grasps the place of divine revelation in the life of the mind, and once one acknowledges the significance of canonical or corporate decisions in the life of our Church, one can surely begin to see why the debate about homosexuality cuts so deeply. I will not here speak for liberals, but I think I do understand the intellectual and spiritual impulses that, for better or worse, undergird the conservative defense of *The Book of Discipline*. Now I am aware that our convictions and the way we hold them are shot through with all sorts of distortion, sin, cultural baggage, personal prejudice, and the like. Yet on the matter before us, conservatives are both tenacious and urgent. This is not accidental. They are tenacious because the position they hold is not just a matter of human judgment or opinion. It is construed as the teaching of our Lord in divine revelation. They are urgent because they believe that the rejection of divine revelation involves the unraveling of the fabric of faith and the radical undermining of the canonical commitments of The United Methodist Church. For better or worse, they foresee chaos and division if the position of *The Book of Discipline* were revised.

It is a very serious mistake to reduce this tenacity to lust for power; politics; conventional, bourgeois morality, homophobia, white male patriarchy; and the like. At one level, what is at stake is the measure of cognitive dissonance any community can endure. Surely judgments about potential division need to be weighed carefully and systematically. It is at least likely that those who support the current position of the Church on homosexuality would find it extremely difficult to remain within the Church they love should the position of *The Book of Discipline* on homosexuality be changed.

Much more important is that what is at stake are the foundations of the Church in the Word of God and the place of The United Methodist Church within the church catholic and apostolic. This matter is equally important in any effort to make sense of the convictions of serious conservatives within The United Methodist Church. With this we turn more directly to the issue of ecclesiology.

Revelation and the Nature of the Church

It is a commonplace to claim that United Methodists are thoroughly confused in their doctrine of the Church. Yet whatever confusion we find among members and among theologians, there is a relatively clear vision of the Church in the Articles of Religion and the Confession of Faith that ties our ecclesiology directly to the foregoing discussion. The United Methodist Church holds that the Church is made of those faithful congregations among which the pure Word of God is preached and the sacraments are properly administered.[27] However we enrich this claim, say, by drawing on features of Methodism as a renewal and reform movement or by highlighting aspects of Wesley's comments on the Church or by adding important new insights that have emerged from our history and current experience, this proposal remains the central claim of our tradition. Nothing else ranks higher in the canonical commitments of our Church. The proper and appropriate preaching of the Word of God and the right administration of the sacraments are critical marks of the Church.

Moreover, this crucial theological marker, the preaching of the Word of God, undergirds both the balance between preaching and sacraments in our practices and the central place of Scripture in the tradition as a whole. We do not, of course, have here in our constitutional articles a full-scale ecclesiology. Thus we do not have any vision of the purpose or mission of the Church; nor do we have answers to pressing questions about the current divisions of the church, about its visibility and invisibility, about the classical marks of the Church as one, holy, catholic, and apostolic. Nor, interestingly, do we have anything on the place of discipline in the life of the Church.[28] These matters are taken up in various doctrinal sites of the Church, but they are not covered by our fundamental doctrine as expressed in the Articles of Religion or Confession of Faith.

These lacunae should not trouble us in the current debate in that they cannot touch what is pivotal in our doctrine, namely, the appropriate preaching of the pure Word of God. The crucial point is this: If The United Methodist Church were to abandon its current teaching on homosexual behavior, it would cease to be a body of congregations among which the pure Word of God is preached; and thus it would undermine its own most important ecclesiological insight. Expressed positively, there is a happy correlation and consistency between the position of The United Methodist Church on homosexuality and its central ecclesiological commitments.[29]

Conclusion

It is the mark of a robust and mature church that it be able to articulate its position on controversial but critical issues in a relatively clear, sophisticated, sensitive, and self-consistent manner. We have seen that this applies to the position of The United Methodist Church in its teaching on homosexuality. That position is neither homophobic nor narrow; it is neither superficial nor simple; it is neither naïve nor hastily developed. On the contrary, it is carefully nuanced, complex, informed, substantive, and refined. Moreover, its formal teaching fits squarely with its commitment to the place of divine revelation in arriving at its central theological and moral commitments and with its core ecclesiological insights.

It is also a mark of a robust and mature church that it be prepared to subject its teaching to serious investigation and scrutiny and that it be open to fresh insights and new truth that may emerge on its pilgrim journey of faith. This too applies to The United Methodist Church in its approach to the topic of homosexuality. It set up a study commission and conducted formal dialogues, in which all parties to the discussion have had a say in the debate. The matter has been pursued at all recent General Conferences. All sides continue to discuss the relevant issues with all the passion, intelligence, and infirmity that are our condition even in the life of faith.

It is a further mark of a robust and mature church that it stand firm on those commitments that have been recognized, however falteringly, as derived from God's special revelation in Christ. This too is true of The United Methodist Church. It has sought to be faithful to its Lord and Savior in its teaching on sexuality, whatever that may cost it in terms of popularity or acceptance in either popular or elite culture. Under the grace of God, The United Methodist Church can continue to stand firm. Indeed, it can do no less, given its clear ecclesiological commitments on the place of the Word of God in its regular proclamation and in its ongoing integrity as a connection of faithful congregations.

CHAPTER 2

The Church — The Vow — The Witness

Bishop Robert E. Fannin

When asked to share my thoughts and feelings surrounding the church and the issue of homosexuality, I am always hesitant. The reluctance is because this issue is so volatile that persons on either side of the discussion are easily misunderstood. Another reason is that I have so many dear friends who are homosexual or who have family members living the homosexual lifestyle. After considerable struggle, I made the decision to write this chapter because my life and ministry have been built around the concept of an open life that has allowed me to share my feelings and understandings on any issue freely and honestly. What follows is not an argument but my witness as a person of deep Christian faith and a bishop of the United Methodist Church concerning this tender matter.

At the very heart of my personality is what may seem very simplistic to many but profound to me as I have made decisions in my life. That is, you would never knowingly make a commitment to, or have a covenant relationship with, someone who violates your very basic understanding of truth, honesty, and respect for others. I have often said that if I ever write a book about relationships, it will most likely be entitled *Respectfully Yours*. This does not mean that you do not disagree or challenge, for relationships are built on new experiences; and as a person or situation changes, so will the covenant. It does mean, however, that you must be faithful to the promises, vows, commitments, and standards of the relationship.

Another tenet of my life has always been to ground all of my words and actions in Holy Scripture. Having served in large diverse communities both in culture and language, it became very important that I not be seen as a person that just changes to fit the moment but would be respected for presenting myself and my faith with clarity and conviction. In other words, it is important that what a person sees and hears from my witness be the same regardless of the circumstances. As we would say back in my hometown, I never want to be seen as a "fair weather friend." This in no way curtails change. I believe that we must always be open to new information and be willing to change as God's creation is constantly being revealed to us. Change not for change's sake, but change that leads us Godward. It is for me, therefore, important to live a life based in Scripture. I will not attempt to detail the biblical material that relates to homosexuality, for others will do so; however, it is important to note that my life, witness, and words are based on my discernment of the Holy Scriptures.

I recently had a person of deep convictions say to me, "Bob, you would change your stand on this matter if you only knew some persons who are homosexuals." I want to make it very clear that I have a number of homosexual friends and colleagues and have very close friendships with persons who have a child, brother, sister, or a very good friend following this lifestyle. I have defended the rights of these and all individuals at different times in my life. While I was the pastor of a university church, it was part of my responsibility to relate to the homosexual community as liaison between the religious community and the university. In a recent meeting, a leading educator said to me, in speaking of homosexual persons he had been associated with, "These are some of the most gifted and talented people I know." He went on to say, "and they are extremely sensitive." I did not disagree with him for that has been my experience as well.

We all are outraged when news reports make us aware of violence perpetrated against persons of homosexual lifestyles. Our *Discipline* strongly rejects such intolerance and injustice. I wanted to emphasize strongly that persons I encounter who support the Church's position—that the practice of homosexuality is inconsistent with Christian teaching—are not "homophobic" and do not wish harm or ill upon anyone. In conjunction with their understanding of Scripture, these people believe in accepting the authority of the Church and respecting the results of its deliberative process that forms our positions stated in the *Discipline*.

Regarding people on various sides of this and other issues, I am thankful for our United Methodist commitment to "holy conferencing." In contemporary terms, we are always willing to have the conversation, to talk and to listen, to have respectful dialogue. We believe the Holy Spirit moves when persons are allowed to express their opinions and differences. I confess that sometimes I wish we could just say, *Enough is enough! Until there is new information beyond what we keep going round and round about, let's move on to other vital matters before the church.* This is, however, not our tradition. We continue to talk and to listen. *In all things, charity.*

Within the life of the Church, the issue of ordination is foremost in our consideration of the practice of homosexuality. Several years ago, I was strongly in favor of commissioning the Committee to Study Homosexuality. By examining the findings of those who study the psychosocial and psychobiological nature of human life and sexuality, the committee, I hoped, could bring some new, decisive information to us. In the end, I was disappointed that the committee itself was strongly divided in its conclusions over the nature of homosexuality.

My conviction is that we do not change the standards of the Church and our understanding of Scripture on information that at best is an "I think so" or "It seems to me." Not long ago, I attended a forum, at which experts made presentations concerning the nature of homosexuality. On the one hand, one speaker said, "It appears to me that one inherits this sexual orientation." On the other hand, I have read books and articles that describe how persons can and do make choices regarding their sexual orientation. In my counseling experience, I know of persons who have changed from a homosexual lifestyle to a heterosexual lifestyle of marriage and parenthood. My purpose here is not to argue the pros and cons, but to call attention to the continued lack of clarity around this issue.

This brings us to my understanding of authority in the life of the church. The authority of the church without question has waned in the last few years. As an episcopal leader, I can testify that the church today in no way is a top-down administration. I personally am very supportive of this turn in direction even though it makes my job much more difficult. I believe we have moved into the "team" era of our life together. We listen, discern, and make decisions not on titles, but on what is best for the church. This is an extremely important segment of the life and authority of the church. In the wise knowledge of those who preceded us, it was determined that the collective body (General Conference) must have the final word. The *Discipline* and the standards for the life of the church must come from those who are chosen to represent the vast body of believers. Even with the faults of a democratic process, it is still by far the most representative of all structures. It has often been said that The United Methodist Church is more democratic than any other organization.

The idea of The United Methodist Church having a president or bishop in charge has often been discussed. Maybe that will be a reality someday; however, here in this day the duly elected body at every level of our Church makes the decisions of ministry and fiscal responsibility. It has been my experience that certainly the church has not always made the right decision, but it is my belief that the spirit of God has been present in that process and my personal opinion is not superior to the authority of the body of believers. This is a crucial theological point as we consider the matter at hand. This issue has been before the church since its creation, and the stand has remained stable and steadfast following numerous studies and countless discussions. I had the opportunity for which I am extremely grateful to be involved in broad discussions around the knowledge surrounding homosexuality and included in personal interviews and discussions with those professing homosexuality as their lifestyle. In that same arena I have spent time with persons who have in their words overcome homosexuality. The church has determined that the information presented thus far is not sufficient to change the church's long-held understanding.

Truth is at the very center of our lives as Christians, and "The truth shall make you free." The search for truth must never end. As I have indicated earlier, I pray for new information that would cast light on homosexuality. There would be a tremendous impact on the life of the church resulting from the churches action on this matter. In the new book *Where the Spirit Leads*, James Rutland Wood writes, "More than one-fourth of U.S. delegates say they feel strongly enough [if the wording of the *Discipline* is changed] to leave the UMC! Thirteen delegates (about 2 percent U.S. delegates) say they would leave if the UMC does not become more accepting of homosexual persons."[1] Can our minds even encompass the magnitude of the effect on the mission, ministry, and life of the church around the world with the potential of those committed laity and clergy represented by one fourth of our United States delegates leaving the body of believers? This is not even taking into consideration the strong response to this issue that has and is being expressed by the global community. The truth is the truth; I would never support anything less; however, the church has spoken that the information known to the body is not sufficient to change the centuries-old belief and practice of the church.

The 2000 edition of *The Book of Discipline of The United Methodist Church* states very clearly, "Homosexual persons no less than heterosexual persons are individuals of sacred worth. All persons need the ministry and guidance of the church in their struggles for human fulfillment, as well as spiritual and emotional care of a fellowship that enables reconciling relationships with God, with others and with self." There is no question in my mind that everyone is entitled to share in the fellowship of the Church. There is no one outside the love and forgiveness of God through Jesus Christ. The place that the Church has taken its stand is around the standards for ordination. This is where I feel that the Church is correct in its obligation to set standards for ministry. It has often been suggested that this should be of no concern because each Annual Conference has the right to set the standards of ministry for ordination within that Annual Conference. In other words, the connection is broken. I cannot tell you the number of times that, in writing for a transfer of an ordained minister from another Annual Conference, the Bishop of the transferring conference has said to me when I ask him or her questions about the person being transferred, "Bob, an ordained minister in one conference is an ordained minister in all conferences." To consider broadening the differences between conferences in setting the standards for ministry weakens the connection, one of United Methodism's greatest strengthens.

The church must always set standards and develop theological understanding; if not, we become individual interpreters of the beliefs of The United Methodist Church, picking and choosing what we will support. For example, in recent days it has been exclaimed that around the issue of homosexuality, the Church should not place ministers in such a position that they must choose between their conscience and the *Discipline*. We would all agree, I am sure, that our baptism is a central aspect of our Christian life. In recent days it has become even more profound as we have spent untold study and discussion developing our statement on our theologian doctrine of baptism. We believe as a church that baptism is eternal in nature and there is no circumstance that calls for rebaptism. When I was the pastor of a university church, it was very popular among the students, especially among those who had not been nurtured by their parents through the life of the church, to ask to be rebaptized. Their point was well taken in that they had not been nurtured by their parents in the Christian faith; therefore, they believed that the vows taken by their parents at the time of their infant baptism were never honored. Today, I would not offer baptism to a person who had already been baptized. I would most likely refer that person to the very meaningful service "Reaffirmation of the Baptismal Covenant." Just as we hold fast to the Church's standards and practice of baptism, we give the same faithful obedience to the standards of ordination.

For some, the statements "This is a justice issue!" or "This is a personal, spiritual matter" seem to mean they are exempt from compliance with a particular church doctrine or practice. In response, sometimes one feels it is politically incorrect to say, "The church has prayerfully considered how to respond to this concern—not hatefully or judgmentally, but with agonizing prayer."

Is "ecclesial disobedience" a matter of little consequence? Is every issue solely on its own, with little value placed on the concerns and understanding of the majority of the church body of believers? Yet again, I affirm our Methodist practice of ongoing respectful conversation over tender and controversial matters. In the meantime and through the process, however, we are faithful by honoring the due process decisions the church has carefully and prayerfully made thus far.

I am writing these words just ten days following the horrendous acts of terrorism in New York, Washington, D.C., and Pennsylvania on September 11. In researching the social principles of The United Methodist Church, it is very clear that we as a body of believers have made a strong statement concerning war. *The Book of Discipline* states, "We believe war is incompatible with the teachings and example of Christ. We therefore reject war as a usual instrument of national foreign policy and insist that the first moral duty of all nations is to resolve by peaceful means every dispute that arises between or among them."[3] This is another standard of the church by which we would expect all clergy and laity to endorse and proclaim. I would certainly instruct and expect all pastors to proclaim peace as the only avenue to reconciliation.

Although I may be overworking my point, there is one experience coming out of my own ministry that reflects light on the discussions surrounding the church and its obligation to set certain standards and principles that clergy and laity should strive to follow. I was appointed to a large church of around three thousand members; when I arrived I discovered that in that community of faith were approximately three hundred persons who claimed to be part of a charismatic movement. They were very supportive of the local church and the greater United Methodist Church. They were so affirming of my ministry that I would often say, "Be careful what you ask for in terms of resources or spiritual enrichment, for if they hear you, it will probably appear the next day." In their gathering they would practice the gift of speaking in tongues, being slain in the spirit, and great sounds of praise. On several occasions they came to me and asked if they could practice some of these gifts in the traditional worship services of the Church. The discussions would get rather involved, but never disrespectful. The conversations would usually end with a strong affirmation of the faith that we shared together in Jesus Christ. Sharing with them the tradition of worship that is outlined in *The Book of Worship* and *The United Methodist Hymnal,* I would decline their request. I always had to make sure that I was not judging a service as a charismatic service when in reality it was an old-fashioned United Methodist evangelical service. The Church must recognize its tradition and set certain standards.

The system of the church allows for great flexibility. From the local church Pastor Parish Relations Committee, to the District Committee on Ordained Ministry and the Conference Board of Ordained Ministry, decisions are made in part based on the interview as perceived by the committee or board members present. There must be, of course, some standards that are set and met across the entire life of the church. These are outlined throughout the *Discipline* and guidelines of the whole body.

This brings us to the very important point of the vows of the church and what part they play in our understanding of the issue of homosexuality. I can remember with great clarity the occasions

38

of my ordination as a deacon, elder, and my consecration as a bishop. The time of examination, the placing of hands on my head, the sacred moments of prayer, and the reading of Holy Scripture was for me an act second only to my baptism. The question was asked, "In covenant with other elders, will you be loyal to the United Methodist Church, accepting its order, liturgy, doctrine, and discipline, defending it against all doctrine contrary to God's Holy Word, and accepting the authority of those who are appointed to supervise your ministry?" My voice trembling, I answered, "I will, with the help of God." Later, in the Order for the Consecration of Bishops, when I was instructed to remember with the words "to reaffirm the vows made at your ordination as elder," memories of the earlier commitment flooded my soul once again. We take many vows in our lives: vows of marriage, friendship, faith, and citizenship. It is extremely important that vows are not taken lightly, but with a commitment that spans the deepest caverns and the highest mountains of our experience. Vows of ordination to support the church and Holy Scripture are sacred.

Adam Hamilton, in his new book, *Confronting the Controversies*, makes a profound statement after thoroughly examining both sides of this tough issue when he says, "Yes I believe homosexual practice is not God's will for us. But homosexual people, I believe you have a special place in God's House, at God's table, in God's service, God knows your struggles and feels your pain. God has heard every prayer you have prayed."[4] Once again, I must reemphasize that for me a major issue in this conversation is the matter of ordination. I would add, based on the present information from various *Disciplines*, the standards set by the church, and the testimony of Holy Scripture, that a self-avowed practicing homosexual would not qualify to be a candidate for ordained ministry.

There is no doubt that we are all sinners and need the forgiveness of God through Jesus Christ. The turning point that leads us closer to God comes when we choose to denounce our sins and vow to lead a new and different life.

I close with a prayer, asking God to continue to give us guidance around this issue, revealing wisdom in the midst of our prayerful conversations. I would also pray that we as a church, in the midst of our struggle, not let the other aspects of our ministry stumble. We are called to serve others, to be constantly immersed in the practice of evangelism, to proclaim the good news of Jesus Christ around the world, and to work toward peace on earth. There is a real danger that we become so issue oriented that we lose our primary commitment to discipleship. My prayer is that The United Methodist Church will continue to set standards based on Holy Scripture for the Christian life in an ever-changing world.

CHAPTER 3

Ecclesial Disobedience or Ecclesial Subordination to Liberal Institutions?

D. Stephen Long

The question of homosexuality has not always been defined in terms of the political right versus the political left. In 1953, the philosopher Michel Foucault left the Communist Party. One of the reasons he did so was because the party taught that homosexuality was a "bourgeois decadence."[1] Homosexuality was associated with the kind of "liberalism" that prohibited the common ownership of property because sexual activity, like economic activity, was viewed as an individual possession to be disseminated irrespective of communal interests. Marx skewered this kind of liberalism, by which "liberty, equality and property" determined economic exchanges. "There alone rule Freedom, Equality, Property and Bentham" wrote Marx, "because each looks only to himself. The only force that brings them together and puts them in relation with each other, is the selfishness, the gain and the private interests of each."[2] It needs little argument to suggest that sexual exchanges—homosexual and heterosexual—in the late modern era have become deeply formed by the liberal, capitalist exchanges against which Marx raged. One could easily replace the term "commodity exchange" in Marx's *Capital* with "sexual exchange" and have an accurate picture of sexuality as depicted in modern culture. But although this seems to me to be obvious, recent Church conversations on questions of sexuality have made little to no mention of the social and political contexts that influence all forms of exchange at present. In fact, many of the arguments for gay and lesbian unions assume the normativity of those forms of exchange and invite the Church to become more accommodated to them, thereby subordinating the Church's theological tradition to that particular tradition of thought and practice known as "liberalism."

"Liberalism" is both a political theory and a practice that privileges individual possession over any communal ownership. It assumes what the individual possesses should be protected against any intrusion of common interests—whether that possession be property, rights, knowledge, or sexual orientation. It was first a system of economic exchange that came to dominance in the eighteenth century. But it is also a system of cultural exchange that defines not only market transactions, but also political and knowledge exchanges. The institutions of modern political governance and education produce the theory and perpetuate the practices that ensure the ongoing tradition of liberalism. As a form of exchange, liberalism constantly encroaches upon all forms of social communication, including family and ecclesial life. If we fail to note this in our current conversations over sexuality in general and homosexuality in particular, we will fail in our vocation as Christians to discern the times in which we live.

This essay will seek to discern those times by first delineating how liberal exchanges are perpetuated in dominant institutions such as the market, democratic government, and the university. The discourse these institutions assume and perpetuate will then be compared to the present state of the question concerning gay and lesbian unions in the life of The United Methodist Church. I will then suggest that the tradition of liberalism has informed the contemporary ecclesiology of United Methodism through its dogmatic commitment to an "inclusivist" Church. This ecclesiology safeguards the tradition of liberalism by policing against any possible form of communal discipline. Only after the development of all these stages will my own faithful support for the Church's prohibition against the blessing of same-sex unions make sense.

1. Liberalism and Its Institutions

Market

In 1776, a revolution occurred in human thought and practice. Adam Smith published his *Wealth of Nations*, which argued that market exchanges should be based on "perfect liberty." Smith is well known for arguing against governmental interference in economic transactions. Less well known is that Smith recognized that the first stage in freeing the market from governmental interference was to free it from the Church. Only after the ties between the clergy and the poor were severed through English usurpation of the Catholic Church's property was it possible for economic exchanges to be rationalized on the basis of liberty rather than Christian charity.[3]

Smith argued that the market should be freed from not only political interference, but also ecclesial interference. In so doing, he created a tradition, which became known after him as "philosophical radicalism," but today is called "neoliberalism." Jeremy Bentham was a caretaker of this tradition. He intensified the call for freedom within which exchanges should occur by challenging any moral principle regulating economic exchanges other than what two people mutually desired. "No man of ripe years, and of sound mind," wrote Bentham, "ought out of lovingkindness to him, to be hindered from making such bargain, in the way of obtaining money, as, acting with his eyes open, he deems conducive to his interests."[4] This liberal tradition was passed on in the twentieth century by persons who are now called "neoconservatives." For instance, in 1944, Friedrich Hayek published his *Road to Freedom*. Given the totalitarianisms of the twentieth century, Hayek thought the only way to preserve freedom was to avoid any imposition of a common life on people. No common end to economic life should be set forth, and no common "end" to the religious or moral life should be established either. Each individual should be given the liberty to define her or his own ends without interference from government or church. As Hayek put it, "the individual should be allowed, within defined limits, to follow their own values and preferences rather than somebody else's."[5]

Morality and theology are, for Hayek, like commodity exchanges, primarily understood as "values and preferences."

This tradition of liberalism now dominates the way the majority of the world's people eats, clothes itself, finds shelter, seeks entertainment, and (most unfortunately) worships. It requires that no "common end" should define a peoples' life, but an individual's rights, preferences, and orientations should be safeguarded against communal encroachments. All common ends are a priori identified as "totalitarianisms." Each individual must decide for himself or herself what his or her end is. Thus, this tradition assumes that an individual's will gives "value" to the world in terms of both economic exchanges and moral, political, and sexual exchanges.

Although this tradition passes itself off as "inclusive," "open," and "tolerant," it hides the exclusionary basis upon which it is predicated. For instance, Milton Friedman wrote the introduction to the fiftieth anniversary edition of Hayek's *The Road to Freedom* and stated, "The socialists in all parties to whom Hayek dedicated his book must once again be persuaded or defeated if they and we are to remain free men."[6] By that comment, Friedman lets us know how serious he and this tradition are. The individual freedom liberalism secures requires the vanquishing of all who would find solace in the practices of a common life. The liberal, open society too readily seeks the destruction of those who do not fit. This helps explain the odd contradiction that the more a society claims to be "liberal and open" the more it arms itself and uses large portions of its income on military spending, building prisons, and incarcerating its citizens.

Educational Institutions

Smith recognized that for his "perfect liberty" to be enacted, changes were necessary both in the notion of political governance and in the educational system. His revolution had the benefit of calling for universal education, but this education was not to be primarily in morality or theology. He defined "the most essential parts of education" as "to read, write, and account."[7] For the free market to effect its perfect liberty, Smith even entertained the possibility that these "essential elements of education" be "imposed" upon the populace:

> The public can impose upon almost the whole body of the people the necessity of acquiring those most essential parts of education, by obliging every man to undergo an examination or probation in them before he can obtain the freedom in any corporation, or be allowed to set up any trade either in a village or town corporate.[8]

The "public" must direct its resources to educate persons in the rationality inherent in the system of exchanges Smith's "perfect liberty" requires. Smith's principles for education receive fuller articulation in J. S. Mill's "application" of the principles to educational systems. Like Smith's work on exchanges and education, Mill's work also contains some important contributions that make our daily exchanges—including intellectual ones—better. He insisted on the education of children as an essential part of what it meant to be a parent (particularly a father). He advocated for women's rights and access to education and challenged the "despotic power of husbands over wives."[9] All this was not new; such calls were present before Mill. But for Mill, these calls arose from his tenacious adherence to liberty as the principle upon which all exchanges should take place. Thus, he also argued that not only "fornication" and "gambling," but also "pimping" and "keeping a gambling house," could be tolerated. He noted that neither should society proscribe for individuals even on these disputed issues, nor should powerful persons be permitted to entice persons into such activities. The individual must be free to enter into such exchanges "either wisely or foolishly, on their own prompting, as free as possible from the arts of persons who stimulate their inclinations for interested purposes of their own."[10]

This reveals another contradiction in the liberal tradition: People must be free to enter into exchanges based on their own self-interest, but no person can impose his or her self-interest on another. One must "convince" the other that it is in her or his interest to engage in the exchange. Once exchanges are based on this underlying principle of liberty, self-interest contradicts itself. It must, at the same time, be and not be the basis for exchange. All communal arrangements must now appear (albeit illusory) as neutral mechanisms, whereby those who exercise them do so without interest. But that, of course, only creates suspicion. In fact, the suspicion against any communal forms of life now becomes the only legitimate form of communal life. This form of exchange has tremendous influence on current university life. The university is viewed as a "neutral" broker of knowledge where individuals come to a marketplace of ideas and are presented with a cafeteria-style approach to "truths," from which they can each choose for themselves. Interference from institutions like the church, synagogue, or mosque cannot be granted a place within universities as they are presently constituted, except on the margins of their life. For these other institutions assume knowledge of truth that is not a function of individual preference. Corporations, however, are given free range within modern universities.

Political Exchanges

The individual will, with its preferences, values, and orientations, becomes the only possible political agent within this liberal tradition. No other account of political agency is countenanced. Of course, this notion of political society finds its preeminent articulation in the United States Declaration of Independence and its opening salvo, "We hold these truths to be self-evident, that all men are created equal, that they endowed by their Creator . . ." Each individual is endowed with a "possession" that must be protected, and it alone can be the basis for political society. But what is the foundation for such a thought? Is it grounded in truth or simply in the fact that this is what we *want* to believe? If it is grounded in a "truth," then something is present outside the individual's will that forms the basis of political society, to which political society would be held accountable. But if we just *will* this political society into being, no such accountability is necessary. As many political theorists have pointed out, this opening salvo is mired in ambiguity.

John Courtney Murray explained the ambiguity this way, "do we hold these truths because they are true or are these truths true because we hold them?"[11] He recognized that if the latter holds, then truth is nothing more than a "value" that our will gives to things such that "truth" was finally a noble illusion. The values of our political society, like the values of SUVs and cappuccinos, are nothing other than an aggregation of individual preferences.

Murray desperately tried to ground American democracy in something other than the individual will to power, and so he

46

argued that the Catholic doctrine of the natural law, which was separable from any theological doctrines, was the true basis for the "American proposition." But as Michael Baxter has noted, Murray grounds the American proposition in the natural law because he finds in the latter a politics "not based on a view of the end of human society and therefore . . . can exclude all controversy over final or ultimate ends."[12] Murray's "natural law" is made to fit the liberal tradition. His Catholic defense of the American proposition stands easily within those forms of exchange that have come to us through Smith, Bentham, Mill, Hayek, and Friedman. But as Baxter also notes, this defense finally invites Catholic Christians to disappear into America by taking on its forms of exchange and to live the illusion that they can do so without any sense of contradiction.

Murray's defense will not stand up to historical scrutiny. A common ecclesial faith and the principle of liberty as articulated in the tradition of liberalism do not easily coexist. As James Madison's "Memorial and Remonstrance Against Religious Assessments" notes, this principle of liberty is based not only on the assumption that the State should not impose a religion on the populace—a principle most of the Christian tradition would agree with to some degree—but also on the assumption that religion *can only be a matter of individual choice, preference, or orientation.* Madison wrote,

> The Religion then of every man must be left to the conviction and conscience of every man; and it is the right of every man to exercise it as these may dictate. This right is in its nature an unalienable right. It is unalienable; because the opinions of men, depending on the evidence contemplated by their own minds, *cannot* follow the dictates of other men.[13]

Madison does not argue that religion *should* not be a communal enterprise, by which we learn obedience to a common life; he argues religion *cannot* be this. It is not possible based upon the principle of individual liberty he has inherited. We are first individuals who possess ourselves before we can be anything else.

To justify their presence within this kind of politics, religious communities must convince the authorities that they stand for something more than obedience to a common life and the preservation of a tradition. The need for this justification is now enshrined in American law because of the 1971 Supreme Court decision known as the *Lemon* test. This decision determined on what basis public aid could be given to so-called parochial or private religious educational institutions. The first of the three *Lemon* tests is that any statute granting such aid "must have a secular legislative purpose."[14] In other words, liberal society supports "private" religious communities only insofar as those communities demonstrate that they have "secular" purpose. Note the language used in the ruling:

> Although the District Court found that concern for religious values did not inevitably or necessarily intrude into the content of secular subjects, the considerable religious activities of these schools led the legislature to provide for careful governmental controls and *surveillance* by state authorities in order to ensure that state aid supports only secular education.[15]

One should not be overly dramatic in reacting against this clear statement of state *surveillance* of religion. The finding calls for surveillance only in the case of "public" expenditures to "private" religious interests. But it does position the state as a neutral arbitrator, ensuring individuals the pursuit of their own values, interests, preferences, and orientations. How far will this surveillance of religious communities extend? Has it so defined our everyday practices that religious communities now practice this surveillance against themselves?

We modern citizens of the United States stand in a clear tradition of liberalism, having been formed in its forms of exchange through market, governmental, and educational transactions. This is not all negative. Inasmuch as a liberal "open society" makes room for persecuted minorities such as gays, Jews, Gypsies, persons of color, and so on, it is clearly preferable to any communist form of governing that subjects such groups to persecution and annihilation. The Church itself has too often sought shelter in the arms of such totalitarian forces, resulting in the problem of "Caesaropapism," in which the government seeks to enforce religious teachings. On many occasions, the results of the marriage of throne and altar were worse than the problems liberalism has generated. If our choice is either a totalitarianism that oppresses, persecutes, and annihilates gay and lesbian persons or a liberalism that allows us each to treat our possessions (including our sexual orientations) as our own property to disseminate as we choose, then surely all right-thinking people will opt for the latter. But is this an adequate either-or, especially when it comes together to think what it means to be the Church? And now that "liberalism" has won and become the only form of exchange that dominates the globe (China alone perhaps being somewhat of an exception), is liberalism itself not tempted to become totalizing, even policing what it means to be the Church?

2. The State of the Question

The dominant argument opposing the United Methodist disciplinary statements against the unions of gay and lesbian persons fits well the tradition of liberalism that defines nearly every cultural exchange at the beginning of the twenty-first century. This argument assumes that the Creator has endowed each individual with a certain orientation that should be protected by right and kept free from encroachment by communal interests. The only moral question is if individuals' choices are authentic expressions of that underlying possession or orientation. This dominant argument for holy unions is set forth under the theological rubric of "creation spirituality." The book *The Loyal Opposition* offers one of the clearest and succinct confessions of this:

> I believe that all of us are created in the image of God, and that God does not make anyone evil or even "incompatible with Christian teaching." I believe that sexual orientation is a good gift of God; the choice we have is how we relate with integrity to ourselves and one another and all of creation through our sexual orientation—whether we are same-gendered or other-gendered in our orientation. If we are forced to be untrue to ourselves, we will tend to be untrue and perhaps abusive to others and to all of creation.[16]

Notice that this is a "creedal affirmation"; it is a statement of belief that assumes our individual sexual orientation is a possession that is a priori good.

Of course, all of the orthodox Christian tradition has affirmed that God only creates what is good, but this good has never been transparent and self-evident. We also recognize that the good often eludes us and that we are self-deceived as to what it is. There is also a "fall" that comes precisely at the point of the knowledge of good and evil. The loyal oppositionists do not seem to take this into account. Instead, an individual orientation is assumed to be good simply because it is an *individual's* orientation. And this argument appears to be compelling to many people of good faith within the Church at the present moment. It is at this point that we need to "discern the times" and ask, "In what social context can this thought pass as reasonable and true? When did an individual's 'orientation' become a self-legitimating ethical good?" I suggest that this particular argument can only pass as reasonable for persons who stand firmly within the dominant institutions of the liberal tradition and their forms of economic, cultural, political, and sexual exchange. Only those of us formed by the current configuration of the free market, the university as marketplace of ideas, and political society as grounded in an individual's self-possession could possibly assume that the question of "orientation" settles the matter. It is not then surprising that the only remaining question is if we "choose" to live authentically with our individual orientation. That the Church might determine some forms of orientation are incompatible with its common life and others are not is now a priori viewed as oppressive. Like the forms of liberal exchange that dominate the market, the university, and government, sexual exchange is first a question of individual possession that cannot be discerned through a quest for a common life. The only task of the Church is to help people choose to live authentically with their orientation. Only persons formed by the institutions produced in the tradition of Bentham, Madison, and Hayek could find this to be a compelling argument.

Notice how only slight alterations in the quotes already noted within the liberal tradition resonate well with contemporary ecclesial arguments for gay and lesbian unions. Bentham noted:

> No man [or woman] of ripe years, and of sound mind ought out of lovingkindness to him [or her], to be hindered from making such bargain, in the way of obtaining [sexual pleasure], as, acting

with his [or her] eyes open, he [or she] deems conducive to his [or her] interests.

Madison said:

The [sexual practices] then of every man [and woman] must be left to the conviction and conscience of every man [and woman]; and it is the right of every man [and woman] to exercise it as these may dictate. This right is in its nature an unalienable right. It is unalienable; because the [sexual orientation] of men [and women], depending on the evidence contemplated by their own minds, *cannot* follow the dictates of other men [and women].

And Hayek said:

the individual should be allowed, within defined limits, to follow their own values and preferences [with respect to sexual exchanges] rather than somebody else's.

Do the similarities between these arguments and those found by the loyal oppositionists in their argument from "orientation" not tell us something about what social location we inhabit when we make these arguments and find them convincing? Have these arguments become our "scriptures"? this tradition our new ecclesial home? The result of this theology is that the loyal opposition asks us to oppose the Church through acts of ecclesial disobedience and, like previous communities who faced "religious persecution" for their disobedience, to find "shelter in America."[17]

The true crisis United Methodism faces at this present moment is only secondarily related to questions of sexuality. The true crisis is that, given the arguments presented for holy unions and the strategies of protest used to force the Church one way or another, our leaders are evacuating the Church of its tradition and replacing it with the tradition of liberalism and its forms of cultural exchange. We have produced an ecclesiology that fits well with the tradition of liberal exchanges that so thoroughly defines our lives.

The "Inclusivist" Church

Nearly a decade ago, I published a book that examined article 16 of The United Methodist Church's Confession of Faith.[18] This article, which uses the same language as the social principle on homosexuality, states "war and bloodshed are contrary to the gospel and spirit of Christ." Both suggest an "incompatibility" between particular forms of life and our communal obedience to Christ. Article 16 is in principle binding upon all the people called Methodists. I wrote that book fresh out of seminary, not yet finished with my further graduate studies. I had the exuberance of a young Methodist pastor who took seriously the teaching of our tradition that we are a holiness sect striving for perfection through a common discipline. I was somewhat taken aback when the book appeared blurbed by the Mennonite theologian John Howard Yoder, with the following comments: "It is fascinating to observe the tensions that arise in an inclusivist church when a careful theological argument proposes that normative statements, which were intended in a nonbinding hortatory mode, should be taken seriously." Yoder's apparent affirmation of my work left me perplexed. At that time I thought he misunderstood Methodism. Because I assumed Methodism was a holiness sect striving for perfection, I did not see why he thought my argument would cause "tension" for an "inclusivist" church. Nor did I think that the statements in our common Confession were "intended in a nonbinding hortatory mode." How can something called a "confession" be understood as "nonbinding"? The articles were, I wrongly thought, to be guides like the General Rules to be used to produce in us what Mr. Wesley called "holy tempers."

More than a decade later, a youthful Methodist exuberance for a common Christian life has given way to the sober reality that Yoder was right. In fact, I have come to see that he understood The United Methodist Church better than I did. Methodism is an *inclusivist* church, whose leadership seems unwilling to countenance other ecclesiological possibilities. Therefore, the sign that hangs outside many of our churches that they are a "welcoming, open, inclusive" place has become our dogma. We are an "inclusivist" church and that is our dogma.

What could be wrong with being an "inclusivist" church? Once again, if our options are open, inclusive, tolerant, and nonjudgmental versus closed, exclusive, intolerant, and judgmental, then any moral person would opt for the former categories. But the problem with being an "inclusivist" church is that those "included" are only those who are committed to a vision of the church as "open" and "inclusive." This becomes a *common* confession defining our membership. We must *believe* in inclusivity whether we practice a holy appreciation of differences (which I would call catholicity and distinguish from "inclusivity") or not. The result is becoming painfully obvious. Those who do not believe in the "inclusive" vision of the Church are slowly but decisively being excluded, particularly from the leadership of the Church. The fact that many in the leadership cannot see the irony in this exclusion based on a dogmatic belief in inclusivity makes one wonder how completely the liberal tradition, with its hidden exclusionary foundation, has been embodied in the life of the Church.

If a believer thinks of Methodism as a holiness sect striving for perfection based on a common life, this ecclesiology cannot, ipso facto, be "included" once we begin with the notion of the Church as "open" and "inclusive"; for the latter, in keeping with the liberal tradition, refuses to exercise discernment on what is keeping with our common life, except for that act of discernment that categorically states we must not judge about common ends. But this reveals the contradiction present in the "inclusivist" church. Far from being able to include persons other than themselves, the "inclusivists" can only produce a homogenous church with people who think alike and thus have a common life, but now it cannot be named. The "inclusivist church" produces a strong, but not easily challenged, version of a *common* life. We invite other people who are just like us—"open and inclusive." The division within United Methodism is not between one tolerant group who believes in inclusivity—"the inclusivists"—and another intolerant group who eschews difference—"the common life sanctificationists"—it is between two different versions of a common life. What creates the tensions with the "inclusivists," as Yoder duly noted, is that persons committed to an inclusivist Church often lack the ability to realize that their ecclesiological vision is as "exclusive" as the "common life sanctificationists."

Let me give an example. When the book *The Loyal Opposition* was developed, one well-known United Methodist ethicist was contacted to contribute to it. This book, which, as the foreword states, has the purpose of witnessing that "pleasing the Triune God" requires the "inclusion of all people," disinvited this ethicist from contributing when his contribution did not fit with the argument of the "loyal opposition." The inclusivist vision of the Church is finally a vision of a liberal Church for all people, that is, for all people who are liberal. Anyone who is different from this must seek shelter elsewhere.

The inclusivist Church clearly mimics the dominant liberal institutions within North American culture and the forms of exchange they invite us to embody. In an effort to ensure that individuals are "accepted and fully supported" based on what they a priori possess, no common life is permitted. In fact, it is policed against. We are not held accountable for our economic exchanges, nor for our political or sexual exchanges. We are not held accountable because we are more formed by the assumptions of the liberal tradition, whereby each is allowed to choose his or her own good rather than pursue a common quest for the goodness of God rooted in a vision formed by Scripture, tradition, and a common discipline. Even the common task that states that the purpose of the Church is to make disciples for Jesus Christ has been publicly challenged by our episcopal overseers on the basis that it is an "imposed," oppressive norm, to which not all United Methodist Churches adhere.

Although it inevitably practices exclusions, the inclusivist Church asserts that it is nonjudgmental. For instance, a recent news report about the advertisement campaign planned by United Methodist Communications sets forth a strategy for new member recruitment based on billboard slogans such as "I believe none of us is qualified to judge."[19] Of course, this is itself a form of dogmatic judgment. It is a dogma—"I believe"—and it is a judgment— "none of us can judge." As any first-year philosophy student should know, to say "thou shalt not judge" is a judgment. But the judgment in this slogan fits well the exclusionary basis of the inclusivist Church. It excludes any who would argue that one of the Church's tasks is precisely to judge—to make discriminations about what constitutes holy living and what does not. Herein lies the problem with the inclusivist Church and its subordination to liberal social institutions. It constantly passes judgments on others while proclaiming all the more loudly that it does not judge or exclude, but only seeks to include. Thus, it has little capacity for self-critical reflection. That makes the inclusivist Church more dangerous than those other more reasonable ecclesiologies that know they must make judgments that will inevitably exclude so they develop publicly accessible mechanisms by which such judgments are made.

I do not see how The United Methodist Church can overturn its marriage practices and bless gay and lesbian unions without accommodating the Church's tradition more thoroughly to the tradition of liberalism that dominates American culture. Even though "spirituality" has become something of a cottage industry in our culture, these are dangerous times for the possibility of sustaining communal forms of religious life that do not accept the modern liberal norm of "progress," whereby everything must always be "new and improved." Liberalism constantly wages war on the past, trying to sever persons from any historical tradition to force them to be "individuals" who chose for themselves based on their individual possessions. It does so as a tradition. I have no doubt that God will preserve the Church even through these times. But the Church must move into the future, as Gerhard Lohfink so beautifully notes, like someone rowing a boat across a river.[20] We cannot move forward without always looking backward. Only when those who seek to bring changes to our marriage practices can do so by demonstrating continuity with our sacred teachings can we enter into the conversations that still need to take place. The "creation spirituality" that currently dominates the conversation does not maintain that continuity; it replaces it with the continuity of the tradition of the "American proposition." Too much is at stake to alter our historic practices on such thin theological arguments.[21]

CHAPTER 4

Can "Ecclesiastical Disobedience" Serve the Unity of the Church?

Leicester R. Longden

*I*n the months before the General Conference of 2000, numerous books, pamphlets, letters, and videos were sent to General Conference delegates, attempting to persuade them to overturn the stance of The United Methodist Church on homosexuality. Many of these publications chose as their watchword the term "ecclesiastical disobedience" and described their protest in terms of conscientious objection, political resistance, and religious rights. One of the most thorough of these documents was a collection of essays edited by Tex Sample and Amy E. DeLong entitled *The Loyal Opposition*.[1]

This essay attempts to demonstrate that the concept of "ecclesiastical disobedience" is a confusing and incoherent concept unless it is part of a well-developed ecclesial identity and polity. Rather than present one more time the arguments, pro and con, of the traditionalists and the revisionists, I want to step back and look at the ecclesial context in which such arguments are offered. I will attempt to show that the controversy over moral teaching and dissent is not only theologically impoverished but also dangerously overidentified with a civil polity. Finally, I want to challenge both traditionalists and revisionists to move beyond the impasse of the current dialogues and debates toward a conversation about the unity of the Church more thoroughly grounded in trinitarian and christological doctrine.

Is "Ecclesiastical Disobedience" a Coherent Concept?

It is now almost a cliché to say that secular modes of thinking and political habits of behavior have invaded the life of our Church. The mechanics of political protest—adorned with the mantle of "prophetic action"—regularly accompany the conference meetings of our Church.[2] In service to the cause of "full inclusion" for homosexuals, the whole panoply of 1960s activism was brought to bear on the 2000 General Conference in Cleveland: activists wearing symbolic clothing, staging sit-ins, performing street theatre, disrupting public meetings, forcing arrests, and writing letters from jail.

The language of dissent and conscientious objection is now so frequently imported into the community of faith that it is taken for granted. There seems to be little awareness of crucial differences between the decisions made by a church in communion with the intergenerational consensual mind of the church and an organization driven by the negotiated compromises of pluralistic democracy. This is not to say that the voice of protest must never speak within the fellowship of the church. But unless the confusion between civic and ecclesial contexts is identified, we will not be able to develop a discerning view of how doctrine and dissent function to shape and critique the life and mind of the church.

In order for "ecclesiastical disobedience" (ED) to function as a coherent concept rather than a mere slogan of activism, the context of its action needs to be clearly defined. "Civil disobedience" (CD) has in mind the larger good of the civil community on whose behalf the "disobedient" act protests an unjust law. Presumably, ED would have in mind the larger good of the ecclesia for whose sake it protests a particular church law that it finds to be "unjust." In other words, in both cases, the act of dissent is a protest against a law or rule that the dissenter believes contradicts the vision or identity of the community out of which he or she speaks.

The essays in *The Loyal Opposition*, despite their attempt to associate ED with terms such as "prophetic responsibility," "doctrinal faithfulness," and "spiritual discipline,"[3] do little to ground their calls for disobedience in a coherent ecclesiology. Their vocabulary is much more heavily weighted with terms such as "resistance," "religious rights," "subversion," and "dissent."[4]

Take for example the essay by Tex Sample, which introduces the reader to the purpose and thrust of the book. Using political, sociological, and literary categories almost exclusively, Sample calls for "political" and "everyday resistance" to the "official teaching of The United Methodist Church on homosexuality [as a] basic direction needed for the immediate future."[5]

He assumes without argument that the church's "official stance" is "the kind of cultural accommodation that violates the gospel." He then declares that "resistance is a Christian virtue" and calls for Christians to pick up the tools of political resistance.[6]

Or consider Ignacio Castuera's attempt to relate ED to "doctrinal faithfulness" (in chapter 11). He conflates CD and ED in such a way that he can reduce the whole history of Christian faith to a kind of heroic struggle between legalists and resisters, Pharisees and prophets. He cites as the heroes of this struggle Gandhi, Rosa Parks, Martin Luther King, Jr., and Lech Walesa. Castuera mentions Luther and John Wesley, but their contribution to church history is significant in his eyes only to the extent that they were practitioners of ED! In fact, Castuera portrays both Luther and Wesley as legalizers and purveyors of "unjust rules" and were surpassed by those "Methodists [who] became part of the group that forged a new nation dedicated to the proposition that all people are created equal."[7] Castuera seems to think that the freedom of the gospel is merely another variant of liberal democracy.

Sample and Castuera are just two of many writers in *The Loyal Opposition* who make little distinction between CD and ED and assume a kind of identity between the civil and ecclesial communities. It never seems to occur to them that others could see their rhetoric, for all its purported boldness, as a quite obvious form of accommodation to the surrounding culture and its political ethos. (The very title, *Loyal Opposition,* is taken from the tradition of political parties out of power.) Rather than offering theological arguments as to why the community of the baptized should rethink together its stance on what is "incompatible with Christian teaching," they opt for the role of playing the vanguard in a renewed civil rights struggle.

Key theological questions are never asked by *The Loyal Opposition.* For example, is there a difference between a civil polity and an ecclesial polity? Is the identity shaped by the former identical to that shaped by the latter? Does the polity of the Christian community have unique purposes and modes of being?

The polity of a community whose goal is the eschatological kingdom of God is not reducible to the civil polity of a nation state. Eugene F. Rogers Jr. has made this point well:

> There is politics and politics. One concerns the civil polity of the United States, England, or Germany, using the languages of civil rights, religious freedom, and so on. Another polity concerns the kingdom of God, life together with God, the heavenly Jerusalem, the Church militant and triumphant. In Augustinian terms, one is the earthly city, the other the city of God. The two are not opposed. . . . Rather theologians must consider the politics of a community of which God is a member. That polity is defined in terms of its end—its beginning and its eschaton, creation and consummation.[8]

For the reasons given above, we may wonder if the ED of *The Loyal Opposition* is really all that "ecclesiastical." Its thought-forms and practices seem more shaped by the ethos of the surrounding political culture and the civil rights struggles of the 1960s than by any deeply informed theological vision.[9]

The definition of "ecclesia" is particularly vague among the practitioners of ED. Principles of "inclusivism," "pluralism," and "individual rights" rush in to fill the vacuum of an undefined ecclesia. As Geoffrey Wainwright wrote some years ago, "'Inclusivism' and 'pluralism' have become formal ideological substitutes for a true catholicity which is always both substantive and qualitative."[10] One might say that just as the writers of *The Loyal Opposition* tend to substitute the concepts and practices of CD for ED, so they have substituted the principles of pluralism and inclusivism for catholicity.

We must look at several historical and cultural factors that have contributed to this tendency to reduce the church's ecclesial identity and catholicity to secular norms and principles.

Inclusivism as a Challenge to Catholicity

The struggle over moral norms and Christian teaching must be understood against the backdrop of the Church's struggle with modernity. For example, the frequent appeals, on the one hand, to the authority of the *Discipline* and, on the other, to the "right" of conscientious objection to unjust laws, are part of the whole struggle with authority that has characterized modernity as such. As J. A. DiNoia puts it:

> The claim of personal autonomy over against moral, religious and to a lesser extent political authorities constitutes the central dogma of modernity. The exercise of authority is frequently identified with authoritarianism. This pervasive cultural mood gives rise in the religious realm to an antipathy to communal norms of any sort.[11]

Unless we recognize this "pervasive cultural mood" of personal autonomy, we may not be capable of a right discernment regarding the urgency with which fellow United Methodists call for "disobedience" and "resistance" to the communal structures of United Methodism.

A second factor that shapes much of the discussion about ED is the powerful claim that the concept of "inclusivism" has exercised over people who live in liberal democracies. This concept, like that of CD, has become a rallying cry for many Christian activists, but they exhibit little awareness of the theological and ecclesial consequences of elevating this principle to a place of unquestioned priority.[12]

One of the most incisive treatments of inclusivism, and what it "*may* and *may not* mean" for the church is, Alan J. Torrance's remarkable essay: "Towards Inclusive Ministry."[13] Torrance gives a brief history of the term and how it functions within the popular typology of inclusivism, exclusivism, and pluralism. He then shows how this typology has been brought under sharp logical analysis and that the entire typology collapses under such scrutiny.[14]

The most relevant point of Torrance's essay for our purposes here is his account of how the term "inclusivism" has exchanged its descriptive role for an evaluative function:

In our liberal democracy the word "inclusive" has come to be more than a merely descriptive term: it is an evaluative one. "Inclusive" denotes a virtue. By contrast, the word "exclusive" carries strongly pejorative connotations. Whereas 'exclusive' may mean quite simply the neutral, logical characteristic "exclusive of claims to the contrary," when used of religious claims in a multi-religious society it is normally taken to mean "exclusive of persons" thereby denoting an evil akin to racism. To be a *religious* exclusivist, therefore, is to be socially, politically and culturally reprehensible if not potentially subversive.[15]

It is precisely this use of inclusivism as a virtuous attitude that characterizes much of the debate within our church with regard to disputed issues such as homosexuality. The frequent charges about the church's "authoritarianism," "exclusivism," and refusal to "welcome all to the Table" have often been driven more by "political correctness" and a sense of moral superiority than by its attention to the serious theological claims that the community of faith needs to adjudicate.

The habitual moralism of United Methodism is probably shocked by Torrance's claim that rigorous theology and ecclesial identity are "exclusivist," but the shock is due to a moralistic failure to think theologically. Torrance, himself, develops a strong argument that even though Christian faith is "exclusive of incompatible claims," it is also "intrinsically dialogical."[16] He shows, in fact,

> that dialogical inclusivism grounded in a non-pluralist, exclusive series of claims may be more inclusive of persons and more open to ideas than the (supposed) inclusivisms which [have been shown] in any case to be incoherent. In other words, pluralism is not only short on logical correctness; it must ultimately sell short the "political" correctness which drives it![17]

The struggle between authority and autonomy continues to linger in the life of the Church. Various popular notions of inclusivism keep stirring the fires of moralism and civil rights hero worship. But once we gain some distance and perspective on these factors, we can begin to identify the current theological impasse.

Beyond the Impasse

The controversy over moral teaching and public dissent in The United Methodist Church is theologically stalled and pastorally incompetent. The controversy is theologically stalled because it has not opened up a new engagement with the Church's classic moral teaching. Rather, it has focused attention upon the political processes and forms of dissent by which a religious institution may be forced to change its stated rules. It is pastorally incompetent because it has turned the persons at the center of the controversy into victims and caricatured the combatants on both sides as heroes (either of freedom or faithfulness) and villains (either false teachers or oppressors).

One would think that the hotly disputed phrase "incompatible with Christian teaching" would direct attention to the grounds and warrants for authoritative Christian teaching, but this has not happened, for the most part. Traditionalists have stood their ground, appealing to the authority of Christian teaching in the past. Revisionists have argued for dissent on the grounds of various new authorities, experiences, or revelations. The traditionalists accuse their opponents of schism and of departing from the historic and universal church. The revisionists accuse their opponents of oppressing the marginalized and of failing to follow the Spirit's progressive urgings toward inclusivism.

One of the reasons it is so hard to move beyond this impasse is that a political and pluralist mind-set continually keeps United Methodists from doing their theological homework. The contenders in the struggle either spend their energies on winning the vote in Annual and General Conferences, or turn every "dialogue," however officially sponsored, into a quota-built round table, whereby a real theological argument cannot happen.[18] But when the last two General Conferences were given the opportunity to appoint a Doctrinal Commission (where, presumably, the Church could set its best theological and pastoral minds to work), they turned it down.

How is it possible to move beyond this impasse? Although I have been a committed "traditionalist" during my ministry as a pastor-theologian, I have yet to see my fellow traditionalists raise as serious a challenge to the theological impasse before us as the recent book by Eugene F. Rogers Jr., *Sexuality and the Christian Body:*

Their Way into the Triune God.[19] I remain unconvinced by Rogers's "defence of marriage wide enough to include same-sex couples and committed celibates," yet I believe he has raised the theological questions that the church needs to address and is currently avoiding.

Rogers is frank about his own revisionist commitments in the controversial struggles over homosexuality in the church. Yet he addresses what the whole church ought to be looking at: ways that "Christianity may be for or against the body, how marriage might be recovered from individualism for the community [and] revitalized as a locus of sanctification, how the Spirit relates to the interpretation of Scripture."[20]

One of the most helpful aspects of Rogers's work is his analysis and typology of the arguments between liberals and conservatives in the homosexuality debate.[21] In two sections, entitled "How Liberals Hear Conservative Arguments" and "How Conservatives Hear Liberal Arguments," he shows how each side characterizes (and often unknowingly echoes) its opponents in the debate. Rogers comes to the conclusion that "the thrust and counterthrust is mostly a dreary business, often theologically sterile, often engaging in *ad hoc* arguments . . . bedeviled by impatience and charges of question-begging on both sides."[22]

Rogers's analysis of the current arguments tries to develop an "Ethics of Controversy" before moving to his constructive proposals. He argues that Christians' theologically correct orientation is "not gay or straight, conservative or liberal. . . . [It is] ecclesial, an orientation for the Church."[23]

In this way he wants to move beyond the typical arguments of revisionists and traditionalists, as well as modern individualism, to hold together identity and community, salvation, and holiness.[24]

A critique of Rogers's proposals for accepting a doctrine of marriage that includes same-sex couples cannot be offered here. There will need to be extended theological argument to determine whether his proposals are a theological breakthrough, or merely a revisionist attempt to use doctrine as a wax nose, bending it to establish predetermined objectives. But we can admit that Rogers's ecclesial and theological seriousness points beyond the current impasse in a way that our Church desperately needs. Liberals have tended to abandon serious doctrinal questions in their rush to "prophetic action," whereas conservatives have complacently rejected all revisionist proposals. Rowan Williams's warning is appropriate: "The *assumption* that revisionism on one question entails wholesale doctrinal or ethical relativism is dangerous for the future of reasoned Christian disagreement of a properly theological character."[25]

Both conservatives and liberals have largely failed to commit themselves to a substantive inquiry into what the Church "ought to teach." They have preferred to remain in factionalist and partisan struggles to win the Church over to their view of the *Discipline*. As a result, this has pushed the roles of bishops and General Conference to the forefront and emphasized disciplinary rulings and procedures to the neglect of real theological work. It is time for The United Methodist Church to awaken from its pragmatic slumbers, so easily disguised by busy activism. It is time for our Church to strive toward an ecclesial identity less captivated by moralistic and uncritical attachment to the principles of pluralism and inclusivism. It is time for our Church to stop being afraid of doctrine.

The homosexuality debate could be an occasion for the Church to deal with profound and perennial theological issues; but, so far, as Rogers puts it, "traditional and revisionist arguments about the body have proved too easy" because they have not been sufficiently "disciplined by more central doctrines in Trinity and christology, nature and grace."[26]

The way ahead for our Church will require a concerted effort to reclaim our identity as an ecclesial community that has real and identifiable "central doctrines" located in our doctrinal standards. And then, our Church must commit itself to serious theological engagement with these doctrinal standards if we are ever to have the kind of communal discernment that enables us to move beyond our current impasse.

PART II: THE BIBLE

CHAPTER 5

The Biblical Witness Concerning Homosexuality[1]

Richard B. Hays

1. Reading the Texts

*T*he paucity of texts addressing the issue of homosexuality is a significant fact for New Testament ethics. What the Bible does say should be heeded carefully, but any ethic that intends to be biblical will seek to get the accents in the right place. The New Testament emphasizes sharing with the poor and renouncing violence far more than peripheral issues of sexual conduct.

In dealing with homosexuality, we will first comment briefly on the relevant Old Testament texts before turning to the New Testament. This procedure will enable us to clear away some possible misconceptions and to delineate the basis for the traditional Jewish teaching that is presupposed by the New Testament writers.

A. Genesis 19:1-29

The notorious story of Sodom and Gomorrah—often cited in connection with homosexuality—is actually irrelevant to the topic. The "men of Sodom" came pounding on Lot's door, apparently with the intention of gang-raping Lot's two visitors—who, as we readers know, are actually angels. The angels rescue Lot and his family and pronounce destruction on the city. The gang-rape scenario exemplifies the wickedness of the city, but there is nothing in the passage pertinent to a judgment about the morality of consensual homosexual intercourse. Indeed, there is nothing in the rest of the biblical tradition, save an obscure reference in Jude 7, to suggest that the sin of Sodom was particularly identified with sexual misconduct of any kind.[2] In fact, the clearest statement about the sin of Sodom is to be found in an oracle of the prophet Ezekiel: "This was the guilt of your sister Sodom: she and her daughters had pride, excess of food, and prosperous ease, but did not aid the poor and needy" (16:49).

B. Leviticus 18:22, 20:13

The few biblical texts that *do* address the topic of homosexual behavior, however, are unambiguously and unremittingly negative in their judgment. The holiness code in Leviticus explicitly prohibits male homosexual intercourse: "You shall not lie with a male as with a woman; it is an abomination" (18:22). (Nothing is said here about female homosexual behavior.) In Leviticus 20:10-16, the same act is listed as one of a series of sexual offenses—along with adultery, incest, and bestiality—that are punishable by death. It is worth noting that the *act* of "lying with a male as with a woman" is categorically proscribed: Motives for the act are not treated as a morally significant factor. This unambiguous legal prohibition stands as the foundation for the subsequent universal rejection of male same-sex intercourse within Judaism.[3] Quoting a law from Leviticus, of course, does not necessarily settle the question for Christian ethics. The Old Testament contains many prohibitions and commandments that have, ever since the first century, generally been disregarded or deemed obsolete by the church, most notably rules concerning circumcision and dietary practices. Some ethicists have argued that the prohibition of homosexuality is similarly superseded for Christians: It is merely part of the Old Testament's ritual "purity rules" and therefore is morally irrelevant today.[4]

The Old Testament, however, makes no systematic distinction between ritual law and moral law. The same section of the holiness code also contains, for instance, the prohibition of incest (Lev. 18:6-18). Is that a purity law or a moral law? Leviticus makes no distinction in principle. In each case, the church is faced with the task of discerning whether Israel's traditional norms remain in force for the new community of Jesus' followers. In order to see what decisions the early church made about this matter, we must turn to the New Testament.

C. 1 Corinthians 6:9-11; 1 Timothy 1:10; Acts 15:28-29

The early church did, in fact, consistently adopt the Old Testament's teaching on matters of sexual morality, including homosexual acts. In 1 Corinthians 6:9 and 1 Timothy 1:10, for example, we find homosexuals included in lists of persons who do things unacceptable to God.

In 1 Corinthians 6, Paul, exasperated with the Corinthians—some of whom apparently believe themselves to have entered a state of exalted "knowledge," in which the moral rules of their old existence no longer apply to them (cf. 1 Cor. 4:8, 5:1-2, 8:1-9)—confronts them with a blunt rhetorical question: "Do you not know that wrongdoers will not inherit the kingdom of God?" He then gives an illustrative list of the sorts of persons he means: "fornicators, idolaters, adulterers, *malakoi, arsenokoitai,* thieves, the greedy, drunkards, revilers, robbers" (6:9).

I have left the terms pertinent to the present issue untranslated because their translation has been disputed recently by John Boswell and others.[5] The word *malakoi* is not a technical term meaning "homosexuals" (no such term existed either in Greek or in Hebrew), but it appears often in Hellenistic Greek as pejorative slang to describe the "passive" partners—often young boys—in homosexual activity. The other word, *arsenokoitai,* is not found in any extant Greek text earlier than 1 Corinthians. Some scholars have suggested that its meaning is uncertain, but Robin Scroggs has shown that the word is a translation of the Hebrew *mishkav zakur* ("lying with a male") derived directly from Leviticus 18:22 and 20:13 and used in rabbinic texts to refer to homosexual intercourse.[6] The Septuagint (Greek Old Testament) of Leviticus 20:13 reads, "Whoever lies with a man as with a woman *(meta arsenos koitēn gynaikos),* they have both done an abomination." This is almost certainly the idiom from which the noun *arsenokoitai* was coined. Thus, Paul's use of the term presupposes and reaffirms the holiness code's condemnation of homosexual acts.

In 1 Corinthians 6:11, Paul asserts that the sinful behaviors cataloged in the vice list were formerly practiced by some of the Corinthians. Now, however, since they have been transferred into the sphere of Christ's lordship, they ought to have left these practices behind: "This is what some of you used to be. But you were washed, you were sanctified, you were justified in the name of the Lord Jesus Christ and in the Spirit of our God." The remainder of the chapter (vv. 12-20), then, counsels the Corinthians to glorify God in their bodies, because they belong now to God and no longer to themselves.

The 1 Timothy passage includes *arsenokoitai* in a list of "the lawless and disobedient," whose behavior is specified in a vice list that includes everything from lying to slave-trading to murdering one's parents, under the rubric of actions "contrary to the sound teaching that conforms to the glorious gospel."

D. Romans 1:18-32

The most crucial text for Christian ethics concerning homosexuality remains Romans 1, because this is the only passage in the New Testament that explains the condemnation of homosexual behavior in an explicitly theological context:

> Therefore God gave them up in the lusts of their hearts to impurity, to the dishonoring[7] of their bodies among themselves, because they exchanged the truth about God for a lie and worshiped and served the creature rather than the Creator. . . . For this reason God gave them up to dishonorable passions. Their women exchanged natural intercourse for unnatural, and in the same way also the men, giving up natural intercourse with women, were consumed with passion for one another. Men committed shameless acts with men and received in their own persons the due penalty for their error. (Rom. 1:24-27)

(This is, incidentally, the only passage in the Bible that refers to lesbian sexual relations.)

After the greeting and introductory thanksgiving (Rom. 1:1-15), the substance of Paul's exposition begins with a programmatic declaration in 1:16-17: The gospel is "the power of God for salvation to everyone who has faith, to the Jew first and also to the Greek. For in it the righteousness of God is revealed through faith for faith; as it is written, 'The one who is righteous will live by faith.'" This theologically pregnant formulation emphasizes first of all the character of the gospel as an active manifestation of God's power.

Having sounded this keynote, Paul abruptly modulates into a contrasting key by turning to condemn the unrighteousness of fallen humanity: "For the wrath of God is revealed from heaven against all ungodliness and wickedness of those who by their wickedness suppress the truth" (1:18). The Greek word from which the NRSV translates "wickedness" *(adikia)*, used twice in 1:18 for unmistakable emphasis, is the direct antithesis of "righteousness" *(dikaiosynē)*. Humanity's unrighteousness consists fundamentally in their refusal to honor God and render him thanks (1:21). God has clearly shown forth his "power and divine nature" in and through the created world (1:19-20), but the human race in general has disregarded this evidence and turned on a massive scale to idolatry (1:23). The genius of Paul's analysis lies in his refusal to posit a catalog of sins as the cause of human alienation from God. Instead, he delves to the root: All other depravities follow from the radical rebellion of the creature against the Creator (1:24-31). The way in which the argument is framed here is crucial: Ignorance of God is the *consequence* of humanity's primal rebellion.

The passage is not merely a polemical denunciation of selected pagan vices; it is a diagnosis of the human condition. The diseased behavior detailed in verses 24-31 is symptomatic of the one sickness of humanity as a whole. Because they have turned away from God, "all, both Jews and Greeks, are under the power of sin" (3:9).

According to Paul's analysis, God's "wrath" against his fallen human creatures takes the ironic form of allowing them the freedom to have their own way, abandoning them to their own devices: "Therefore God gave them up in the lusts of their hearts to impurity, to the dishonoring of their bodies among themselves, because they exchanged the truth about God for a lie and worshiped and served the creature rather than the Creator" (1:24-25). These and the following sentences, in which the refrain "God gave them up" occurs three times (1:24, 26, 28), repeatedly drive home Paul's point: Idolatry finally debases both the worshiper and the idol. The refusal to acknowledge God as Creator ends in blind distortion of the creation.

Thus, the particular depravities cataloged in verses 24-31 serve two basic purposes in Paul's argument. First, Paul is not warning his readers that they will incur the wrath of God if they do the things that he lists here; rather, speaking in Israel's prophetic tradition, he is presenting an empirical survey of rampant human lawlessness as evidence that God's wrath and judgment are *already* at work in the world. Second, the heaping-up of depravities also serves to demonstrate Paul's evaluation of humanity as deeply implicated in "ungodliness and wickedness" (1:18*b*).

It is certainly true that Paul's portrayal of homosexual behavior is of a secondary and illustrative character in relation to the main line of argument;[8] however, the illustration is one that both Paul and his readers would have regarded as particularly vivid. Rebellion against this Creator who may be "understood and seen in the things that he has made" is made palpable in the flouting of sexual distinctions that are fundamental to God's creative design (Rom. 1:20*b*). The reference to God as creator would certainly evoke for Paul, as well as for his readers, immediate recollections of the creation story in Genesis 1–3, which proclaims that "God created humankind in his image . . . male and female he created them," charging them to "be fruitful and multiply" (Gen. 1:27-28).[9] Genesis 2:18-24 describes woman and man as created for each other and concludes with a summary moral: "Therefore a man leaves his father and his mother and cleaves to his wife, and they become one flesh" (Gen. 2:24). Thus, the complementarity of male and female is given a theological grounding in God's creative activity. By way of sharp contrast, in Romans 1, Paul portrays homosexual behavior as an outward and visible sign of an inward and spiritual reality: the rejection of the Creator's design. Thus, Paul's choice of homosexuality as an illustration of human depravity is not merely random: It serves his rhetorical purposes by providing a vivid image of humanity's primal rejection of the sovereignty of God the creator.

In Romans 1:26-27, however, he introduces a further development in his account of humanity's tragic rebellious trade-off: "Their women exchanged *(metēllaxan)* natural relations for unnatural, and the men likewise gave up natural relations with women and were consumed with passion for one another" (RSV). The deliberate repetition of the verb *metēllaxan* forges a powerful rhetorical link between the rebellion against God and the "shameless acts" (1:27) that are themselves both evidence and consequence of that rebellion.

In describing what it is that straying humans have "exchanged," Paul for the first time introduces the concept of "nature" *(physis)* into the argument (1:26): They have exchanged (translating literally) "the natural use for that which is contrary to nature" *(tēn physikēn chrēsin eis tēn para physin)*. What did Paul mean by "nature," and where does this idea come from?

There are abundant instances, both in the Greco-Roman moral philosophers and in literary texts, of the opposition between "natural" *(kata physin)* and "unnatural" *(para physin)* behavior. These categories play a major role in Stoicism, in which right moral action is closely identified with living *kata physin*. In particular, the opposition between "natural" and "unnatural" is very frequently used (in the absence of convenient Greek words for "heterosexual" and "homosexual") as a way of distinguishing between heterosexual and homosexual behavior.[10]

This categorization of homosexual behavior as "contrary to nature" was adopted with particular vehemence by Hellenistic Jewish writers, who tended to see a correspondence between the philosophical appeal to "nature" and the teachings of the Law of Moses. "The Law recognizes no sexual connections," writes Josephus, "except for the natural *(kata physin)* union of man and wife, and that only for the procreation of children. But it abhors the intercourse of males with males, and punishes any who undertake such a thing with death."[11] In Paul's time, the categorization of homosexual practices as *para physin* was a commonplace feature of polemical attacks against such behavior, particularly in the world of Hellenistic Judaism. When this idea turns up in Romans 1 (in a form relatively restrained by comparison to the statements of some of Paul's contemporaries, both pagan and Jewish), we must recognize that Paul is hardly making an original contribution to theological thought on the subject; he speaks out of a Hellenistic-Jewish cultural context, in which homosexuality is regarded as an abomination; and he assumes that his readers will share his negative judgment of it. Those who indulge in sexual practices *para physin* are defying the Creator and demonstrating their own alienation from him.

Let us summarize briefly our reading of Paul on this issue. The aim of Romans 1 is neither to teach a code of sexual ethics, nor to warn of God's judgment against those who are guilty of particular sins. Rather, Paul is offering a *diagnosis* of the disordered human condition: He adduces the fact of widespread homosexual behavior as evidence that human beings are indeed in rebellion against their Creator. The fundamental human sin is the refusal to honor God and give God thanks (Rom. 1:21); consequently, God's wrath takes the form of letting human idolatry run its own self-destructive course. Homosexual activity, then, is not a *provocation* of "the wrath of God" (Rom. 1:18); rather, it is a *consequence* of God's decision to "give up" rebellious creatures to follow their own futile thinking and desires. The unrighteous behavior cataloged in Romans 1:26-31 is a list of *symptoms:* the underlying sickness of humanity as a whole, of Jews and Greeks alike, is that they have turned away from God and fallen under the power of sin (Rom. 3:9).

Repeated again and again in recent debate is the claim that Paul condemns only homosexual acts committed promiscuously by heterosexual persons—because they *"exchanged* natural intercourse for unnatural." Paul's negative judgment, so the argument goes, does *not* apply to persons who are "naturally" of homosexual orientation. This interpretation, however, is untenable. The "exchange" is not a matter of individual life decisions; rather, it is Paul's characterization of the fallen condition of the pagan world. In any case, neither Paul nor anyone else in antiquity had a concept of "sexual orientation." To introduce this concept into the passage (by suggesting that Paul disapproves only those who act contrary to their individual sexual orientations) is to lapse into anachronism. The fact is that Paul treats *all* homosexual activity as prima facie evidence of humanity's tragic confusion and alienation from God the Creator.

But one more thing must be said: Romans 1:18-32 sets up a homiletical sting operation. The passage builds a crescendo of condemnation, declaring God's wrath upon human unrighteousness, using rhetoric characteristic of Jewish polemic against Gentile immorality. It whips the reader into a frenzy of indignation against others: those unbelievers, those idol worshipers, those immoral enemies of God. But then, in Romans 2:1, the sting strikes: "Therefore you have no excuse, whoever you are, when you judge others; for in passing judgment on another you condemn yourself, because you, the judge, are doing the very same things." The reader who gleefully joins in the condemnation of the unrighteous is "without excuse" *(anapologētos)* before God (2:1), just as those who refuse to acknowledge God are *anapologētos* (1:20). Consequently, for Paul, self-righteous judgment of homosexuality is just as sinful as the homosexual behavior itself. That does not mean that Paul is disingenuous in his rejection of homosexual acts and all the other sinful activities mentioned in Romans 1:24-32; all the evils listed there remain evils (see also Rom. 6:1-23).[12] But no one should presume to be above God's judgment; all of us stand in radical need of God's mercy.

2. Synthesis: Homosexuality in Canonical Context

Though only a few biblical texts speak of homoerotic activity, all that do mention it express unqualified disapproval. Thus, on this issue, there is no synthetic problem for New Testament ethics. In this respect, the issue of homosexuality differs significantly from matters such as slavery or the subordination of women, concerning which the Bible contains internal tensions and counterposed witnesses. The biblical witness against homosexual practices is univocal.

No theological consideration of homosexuality can rest content, however, with a short list of passages that treat the matter explicitly. We must consider how Scripture frames the discussion more broadly: How is human sexuality portrayed in the canon as a whole, and how are the few explicit texts treating homosexuality to be read in relation to this larger canonical framework? To place the prohibition of homosexual activity in a canonical context, we should keep in mind at least the following factors in the biblical portrayal of human existence before God.

A. God's Creative Intention for Human Sexuality

From Genesis 1 onwards, Scripture affirms repeatedly that God has made man and woman for each other and that our sexual desires rightly find fulfillment within heterosexual marriage. (See, for instance, Mark 10:2-9; 1 Thess. 4:3-8; 1 Cor. 7:1-9; Eph. 5:21-33; and Heb. 13:4. The Song of Solomon, however it is to be interpreted, also celebrates love and sexual desire between man and woman.) This normative canonical picture of heterosexual marriage provides the positive backdrop against which the Bible's few emphatic negations of homosexuality must be read.

B. No Essentialism in Gender Orientation

Nowhere does the Bible speak of sexual orientation, nor does it categorize the identity of human beings according to sexual preferences. The tendency to describe sexual orientation as a fundamental "hard-wired" aspect of personhood is a modern development.

C. The Fallen Human Condition

The biblical analysis of the human predicament, most sharply expressed in Pauline theology, offers a subtle account of human bondage to sin. As great-grandchildren of the Enlightenment, we like to think of ourselves as free moral agents, choosing rationally among possible actions; but Scripture unmasks that cheerful illusion and teaches us that we are deeply infected by the tendency to self-deception. As Jeremiah lamented, "The heart is deceitful above all things, and desperately corrupt; who can understand it?" (17:9, RSV). Once in the fallen state, we are not free not to sin: We are "slaves of sin" (Rom. 6:17), which distorts our perceptions, overpowers our will, and renders us incapable of obedience (Rom. 7). Redemption (a word that means "being emancipated from slavery") is God's act of liberation, setting us free from the power of sin and placing us within the sphere of God's transforming power for righteousness (Rom. 6:20-22, 8:1-11; cf. 12:1-2).

Thus, the Bible's sober anthropology rejects the apparently commonsense assumption that only freely chosen acts are morally culpable. Quite the reverse, the very nature of sin is that it is *not* freely chosen. That is what it means to live "in the flesh" in a fallen creation. We are in bondage to sin but still accountable to God's righteous judgment of our actions. In light of this theological anthropology, it cannot be maintained that a homosexual orientation is morally neutral because it is involuntary.

D. Demythologizing Sex

The Bible undercuts our cultural obsession with sexual fulfillment. Scripture (along with many subsequent generations of faithful Christians) bears witness that lives of freedom, joy, and service are possible without sexual relations. Indeed, however odd it may seem to contemporary sensibilities, some New Testament passages (Matt. 19:10-12 and 1 Cor. 7) clearly commend the celibate life as a way of faithfulness. In the view of the world that emerges from the pages of Scripture, sex appears as a matter of secondary importance. To be sure, the power of sexual drives must be acknowledged and subjected to constraints, either through marriage or through disciplined abstinence. But never within the canonical perspective does sexuality become the basis for defining a person's identity or for finding meaning and fulfillment in life. The things that matter are justice, mercy, and faith (Matt. 23:23). The love of God is far more important than any human love. Sexual fulfillment finds its place, at best, as a subsidiary good within this larger picture.

In my book *The Moral Vision of the New Testament,* I suggested that when we seek to understand the New Testament's teaching on any particular question, we must first assemble the relevant texts and then read them through three focal lenses: the images of *community, cross,* and *new creation.*[13] How might these three focal images clarify our interpretation of the New Testament witness concerning homosexuality?

Community

The biblical strictures against homosexual behavior are concerned not just for the private morality of individuals, but for the health, wholeness, and purity of the elect *community.* This perspective is certainly evident in the holiness code of Leviticus. Almost immediately following the prohibition of homosexual conduct (Lev. 18:22) is the following general warning, which refers to all the foregoing rules about sexual practices (Lev. 18:6-23):

> Do not defile yourselves in any of these ways, for by all these practices the nations I am casting out before you have defiled themselves. Thus the land became defiled; and I punished it for its iniquity, and the land vomited out its inhabitants. But you shall keep my statutes and my ordinances and commit none of these abominations, either the citizen or the alien who resides among you. (Lev. 18:24-26)

Israel as a holy nation is called upon, for the sake of the whole people's welfare, to keep God's commandments. Those who transgress the commandments defile not merely themselves, but the whole land, jeopardizing the community as a whole. That is why "whoever commits any of these abominations shall be cut off from their people" (Lev. 18:29).

Similarly, Paul's exhortation to the Corinthians to "glorify God in your body" (1 Cor. 6:20) grows out of his passionate concern, expressed repeatedly in this letter, for the unity and sanctification of the community as a whole. Fornication with a prostitute is wrong because, among other reasons, "your bodies are members of Christ" (6:15). Thus, to engage in sexual immorality defiles the body of Christ. Through baptism, Christians have entered a corporate whole whose health is at stake in the conduct of all its members. Sin is like an infection in the body; thus moral action is not merely a matter of individual freedom and preference: "If one member suffers, all suffer" (1 Cor. 12:26). This line of argument is not applied specifically to every offense in the vice list of 1 Corinthians 6:9-10, but it does not require a great leap of imagination to see that for Paul the church is analogous (though not identical) to Israel, as portrayed in the holiness code. The New Testament never considers sexual conduct a matter of purely private concern between consenting adults. According to Paul, everything that we do as Christians, including our sexual practices, affects the whole body of Christ.

Cross

No New Testament text brings the issue of homosexuality into direct relationship with the story of Jesus' death. The connection is, however, implicit and crucial in Romans. The human rebellion and unrighteousness summarized in Romans 1:18-32 is in fact the condition of crisis that makes the death of Jesus necessary. "God proves his love for us in that while we were still sinners Christ died for us" (Rom. 5:8). The human unrighteousness detailed in Romans 1 is answered by the righteousness of God, who puts forward Jesus to die for the unrighteous (Rom. 3:23-25) and to enable them to walk in newness of life.

> For God has done what the law, weakened by the flesh, could not do: by sending his own Son in the likeness of sinful flesh, and to deal with sin, he condemned sin in the flesh, so that the just requirement of the law might be fulfilled in us, who walk not according to the flesh but according to the Spirit. (Rom. 8:3-4)

What are the implications of this for reading what Romans 1 says about homosexual practices?

First of all, it means that the wrath of God—manifested in God's "giving up" of rebellious humanity to follow their own devices and desires—is not the last word. The gospel of the cross declares that God loves us even while we are in rebellion and that the sacrificial death of his own Son is the measure of the depth of that love. That is the fundamental theological logic underlying Paul's "sting" exposé of self-righteousness in Romans 2:1: We ought not to leap to condemnation of others, for we—no less than those who are engaged in "the dishonoring of their bodies"—are under God's judgment, and they—no less than we—are the objects of God's deeply sacrificial love. This has profound implications for how the Christian community ought to respond to persons of homosexual inclination. Even if some of their actions are contrary to God's design, the *cross* models the way the community of faith ought to respond to them, not in condemnation, but in sacrificial service. This is a particularly urgent word for the church in a time when the AIDS plague has wrought great suffering. (Many members of the gay community have responded to this crisis with actions of self-sacrificial love that authentically reflect the paradigm of the cross; the church at large would do well to learn from such examples.)

Second, the cross marks the end of the old life under the power of sin (Rom. 6:1-4). Therefore, no one in Christ is locked into the past or into a psychological or biological determinism. Only in light of the transforming power of the cross can Paul's word of exhortation be spoken to Christians who struggle with homosexual desires:

> Therefore, do not let sin exercise dominion in your mortal bodies, to make you obey their passions. No longer present your members to sin as instruments of wickedness, but present yourselves to God as those who have been brought from death to life, and present your members to God as instruments of righteousness. For sin will have no dominion over you, since you are not under law but under grace. (Rom. 6:12-14)

Paul's references to homosexual conduct place it within the realm of sin and death to which the cross is God's definitive answer. All of this is simply to say that the judgment of Romans 1 against homosexual practices should never be read apart from the rest of the letter, with its message of grace and hope through the cross of Christ.

New Creation

A similar point can be made here: Neither the word of judgment against homosexual practices nor the hope of transformation to a new life should be read apart from the eschatological framework of Romans. The Christian community lives in a time of tension between "already" and "not yet." Already we have the joy of the Holy Spirit; already we experience the transforming grace of God. But at the same time, we do not yet experience the fullness of redemption: We walk by faith, not by sight. The creation groans in pain and bondage, "and not only the creation, but we ourselves, who have the first fruits of the Spirit, groan inwardly while we wait for adoption, the redemption of our bodies" (Rom. 8:23). This means, among other things, that Christians, set free from the power of sin through Christ's death, must continue to *struggle* to live faithfully in the present time. The "redemption of our bodies" remains a future hope; final transformation of our fallen physical state awaits the resurrection.

3. Hermeneutics: Responding to the Bible's Witness Against Homosexuality

As the foregoing exegetical discussion has shown, Scripture offers no loopholes or exception clauses that might allow for the acceptance of homosexual practices under some circumstances. Despite the efforts of some recent interpreters to explain away the evidence, the Bible remains unambiguous and univocal in its condemnation of homosexual conduct. The difficult questions that the Church must face, therefore, are all *hermeneutical* questions. In what way are we to apply these texts to the issues that confront us at the end of the twentieth century, as the church faces new and forceful demands for the acceptance and ordination of self-described "gay" persons?

One striking finding of our survey of the handful of relevant texts is that the New Testament contains no passages that clearly articulate a *rule* against homosexual practices. The Leviticus texts, of course, bluntly and explicitly prohibit male homosexual acts in a rule form. Paul, as we have seen, presupposes this. In 1 Corinthians 6:9-11, he states no rule to govern the conduct of Christians; rather, he declares that they have already been transferred from an old life of sin to a new life of belonging to Jesus Christ. In other words, he presents a descriptive account of the new symbolic world within which discernments about Christian conduct are to be made.

The New Testament passages in question do express ideas that can be read as *principles* governing sexual conduct. From Romans 1, one could properly infer the principle that human actions ought to acknowledge and honor God as creator. When read against the specific background of the Genesis creation story, this principle yields for Paul the conclusion that homosexuality is contrary to the will of God. This application of the principle, however, is dependent on a particular construal of the order of creation.

Similarly, from the slightly wider context of 1 Corinthians 6, we could derive the *principle*: "Glorify God in your body" (6:20b). Good advice, no doubt, but how does it apply to the issue of our immediate concern? In its original context, the sense of the principle is governed by the more particular specifications of 1 Corinthians 6:9-10 and 6:15-18. If the principle is removed from these moorings, it could mean almost anything up to and including, "Celebrate the divinity of your own body by expanding the horizons of your sexual experience as far as possible." Of course, this would be a complete distortion of Paul's meaning. Thus, we must insist that our interpretation of "biblical principles" be constrained and instructed by the way in which the New Testament writers themselves applied these principles. Specifically, principles such as *love*, *justice*, and *equality* must not be abstracted from their context in the New Testament and employed to justify behavior that the New Testament explicitly condemns.

The only *paradigms* offered by the New Testament for homosexual behavior are the emphatically negative and stereotypic sketches in the three Pauline texts (Rom. 1:18-32; 1 Cor. 6:9; 1 Tim. 1:10). The New Testament offers no accounts of homosexual Christians, tells no stories of same-sex lovers, ventures no metaphors that place a positive construal on homosexual relations. Occasionally, one encounters speculative popular articles that argue Jesus was gay (because of his relationship with the "beloved disciple"; see John 13:23) or that Mary and Martha were not really sisters but lesbian lovers.[14] Such exegetical curiosities, which have found no acceptance among serious New Testament scholars, can only be judged pathetic efforts at constructing a New Testament warrant for homosexual practice where none exists. If Jesus or his followers had practiced or countenanced homosexuality, it would have been profoundly scandalous within first-century Jewish culture. Such a controversy would surely have left traces in the tradition, as did Jesus' practice of having table fellowship with prostitutes and tax collectors. But there are no traces of such controversy. In the paradigmatic mode, the slender evidence offered by the New Testament is entirely disapproving of homosexuality.

A more sophisticated type of paradigmatic argument in defense of homosexuality is offered by those who propose that acceptance of gay Christians in the twenty-first-century church is analogous to the acceptance of Gentile Christians in the first-century church.[15] The stories in Acts 10 and 11 provide, so it is argued, a paradigm for the church to expand the boundaries of Christian fellowship by recognizing that God's spirit has been poured out upon those previously considered unclean. The analogy is richly suggestive, and it deserves careful consideration. The question is whether the analogy is a fitting one and whether it can overrule all the other factors enumerated here that create a strong presumption against the church's acceptance of homosexuality.

The mode in which the New Testament speaks explicitly about homosexuality is the mode of *symbolic world* construction. Romans 1 presents, as we have seen, a portrayal of humankind in rebellion against God and consequently plunged into depravity and confusion. In the course of that portrayal, homosexual activities are—explicitly and without qualification—identified as symptomatic of that tragically confused rebellion. To take the New Testament as authoritative in the mode in which it speaks is to accept this portrayal as "revealed reality," an authoritative disclosure of the truth about the human condition. Understood in this way, the text requires a normative evaluation of homosexual practice as a distortion of God's order for creation.

Likewise, Romans 1 holds abundant resources for informing our understanding of God: God is a righteous God who creates human beings for obedience to his purposes, grants them freedom to rebel, stands in righteous judgment of their rebellion, and manifests his "wrath" by allowing them to suffer the just consequences of their sin. This characterization of God must be held together with the portrayal, developed at length elsewhere in Romans, of God as a merciful God whose righteousness is revealed preeminently in his act of deliverance through Jesus Christ, whose righteousness transforms and empowers us.

Thus, the New Testament confronts us with an account of how the ordering of human life before God has gone awry. To use these texts appropriately in ethical reflection about homosexuality, we should not try to wring rules out of them or abstract principles from them. Instead, we should attend primarily to the way the texts function to shape the *symbolic world* within which human sexuality is understood. If Romans 1—the key text—is to inform normative judgments about homosexuality, it must function as a diagnostic tool, laying bare the truth about humankind's dishonorable "exchange" of the natural for the unnatural. According to Paul, homosexual relations, however they may be interpreted (or rationalized: see Rom. 1:32) by fallen and confused creatures, represent a tragic distortion of the created order. If we accept the authority of the New Testament on this subject, we will be taught to perceive homosexuality accordingly. (Obviously, such a judgment leaves open many questions about how best to deal with the problem pastorally.) Still before us, however, is the problem of how the witness of the New Testament relates to other moral perspectives on this issue. Do we grant the normative force of Paul's analysis?

There are numerous homosexual Christians whose lives show signs of the presence of God, whose work in ministry is genuine and effective. How is such experiential evidence to be assessed? Should we, like the earliest Jewish Christians who hesitated to accept "unclean" Gentiles into the community of faith, acknowledge the work of the Spirit and say, "Who are we to stand in the way of what God is doing?" (Note how this question relates to Peter's experience in Acts 10:1–11:18.) Or should we see this as one more instance of a truth that all of us in ministry know sadly about ourselves: "We have this treasure in earthen vessels"? God gives the Spirit to broken people and ministers grace even through us sinners, without thereby endorsing our sin.

In *The Moral Vision of the New Testament,* I have argued that claims about divinely inspired experience that contradict the witness of Scripture should be admitted to normative status in the church only after sustained and agonizing scrutiny by a consensus of the faithful.[16] It is by no means clear that the community of the church as a whole is prepared to credit the experientially based claims being made at present for normative acceptance of homosexuality. Furthermore, in its rush to be "inclusive," the church must not overlook the *experience* reported by those Christians who struggle with homosexual desires and find them a hindrance to living lives committed to the service of God; nor should it lightly dismiss the testimony of those who claim to have experienced healing and transformation of their sexual orientation. This is a complex matter, and we have not heard the end of it.

In any case, experience must be treated as a hermeneutical lens for reading the New Testament rather than as an independent counterbalancing authority. This is the point at which the analogy to the early church's acceptance of Gentiles fails decisively. The church did not simply observe the experience of Cornelius and his household and decide that Scripture must be wrong after all. On the contrary, the experience of uncircumcised Gentiles responding in faith to the gospel message led the church back to a new reading of the Scriptures. This new reading discovered in the texts a clear message of God's intent, from the covenant with Abraham forward, to bless all nations and to bring Gentiles to worship Israel's God. Only because the experience of Gentile converts proved *hermeneutically illuminating* of Scripture was the church able to embrace Gentiles within the fellowship of God's people. This is precisely the step that has not—or at least not yet—been taken by the advocates of homosexuality in the church. In view of the content of the biblical texts summarized above, it is difficult to imagine how such an argument could be made.

Thus, in view of the considerable uncertainty surrounding the scientific and experiential evidence, in view of our culture's present swirling confusion about gender roles, in view of our propensity for self-deception, I think it prudent and necessary to let the univocal testimony of Scripture and the Christian tradition order the life of the church on this painfully controversial matter. We must affirm that the New Testament tells us the truth about ourselves as sinners and as God's sexual creatures: Marriage between man and woman is the normative form for human sexual fulfillment, and homosexuality is one among many tragic signs that we are a broken people, alienated from God's loving purpose.

References

Boswell, John. *Christianity, Social Tolerance and Homosexuality*. Chicago and London: University of Chicago Press, 1980.

———. *Same-Sex Unions in Premodern Europe*. New York: Villard, 1994.

Boyarin, Daniel. "Are There Any Jews in 'The History of Sexuality'?" *Journal of the History of Sexuality* 5 (1995): 333-55.

Calvin, John. *The Epistles of Paul the Apostle to the Romans and to the Thessalonians*. Calvin's Commentaries, vol. 8, trans. Ross Mackenzie. Grand Rapids: Eerdmans, 1960 [1556].

Countryman, L. William. *Dirt, Greed, and Sex: Sexual Ethics in the New Testament and Their Implications for Today*. Philadelphia: Fortress Press, 1988.

Furnish, Victor Paul. *The Moral Teaching of Paul: Selected Issues*. Rev. ed. Nashville: Abingdon Press, 1985.

Greenberg, David F. *The Construction of Homosexuality*. Chicago: University of Chicago Press, 1989.

Hays, Richard B. "Relations Natural and Unnatural: A Response to John Boswell's Exegesis of Romans 1." *Journal of Religious Ethics* 14 no. 1 (1986): 184-215.

———. *Echoes of Scripture in the Letters of Paul*. New Haven: Yale University Press, 1989.

———. "Awaiting the Redemption of Our Bodies: The Witness of Scripture Concerning Homosexuality." *Sojourners* 20 (July 1991): 17-21.

———. "Justification." In *Anchor Bible Dictionary* 3:1129-33. New York: Doubleday, 1992.

———. *The Moral Vision of the New Testament: Community, Cross, New Creation*. San Francisco: HarperSanFrancisco, 1996.

Johnson, Luke Timothy. *Sharing Possessions: Mandate and Symbol of Faith*, vol. 9. Overtures to Biblical Theology. Philadelphia: Fortress 1981.

———. *Decision Making in the Church: A Biblical Model*. Philadelphia: Fortress, 1983.

Käsemann, Ernst. *Commentary on Romans*. Translated by Geoffrey W. Bromiley. Grand Rapids, Mich.: Eerdmans, 1980.

Laumann, Edward D., John H. Gagnon, et al. *Social Organization of Sexuality: Sexual Practices in the United States*. Chicago: University of Chicago Press, 1994.

Martin, Dale B. "Heterosexism and the Interpretation of Romans 1:18-32." *Biblical Interpretation* 3 (1995): 332-35.

McNeill, John J. *Freedom, Glorious Freedom*. Boston: Beacon Press, 1995.

Porter, Calvin L. "Romans 1:18-22: Its Role in the Developing Argument." *New Testament Studies* 40 (1994): 210-28.

Schütz, John. *Paul and the Anatomy of Apostolic Authority*, vol. 26. Society for New Testament Studies Monograph Series. Cambridge: Cambridge University Press, 1975.

Scroggs, Robin. *The New Testament and Homosexuality*. Philadelphia: Fortress Press, 1983.

Shaw, Brent D. "A Groom of One's Own: The Medieval Church and the Question of Gay Marriage." *The New Republic* 211 nos. 3-4 (1994): 33-41.

Siker, Jeffrey S., ed. *Homosexuality and the Church*. Louisville: Westminster John Knox Press, 1994.

————. "How to Decide? Homosexual Christians, the Bible, and Gentile Inclusion." *Theology Today* 51 no. 2 (July1994): 219-34.

Van Leeuwen, Mary Stewart. "To Ask a Better Question: The Heterosexuality-Homosexuality Debate Revisited." *Interpretation* 51 (1997): 143-58.

van Tilborg, Sjef. *Imaginative Love in John*. Biblical Interpretation Series, 2. Leiden: E. J. Brill, 1993.

Walsh, Jerome T. "Leviticus 18:22 and 20:13: Who Is Doing What to Whom?" *Journal of Biblical Literature* 120 (2001): 201-9.

Wheeler, Sondra Ely. *Wealth as Peril and Obligation: The New Testament on Possessions*. Grand Rapids, Mich.: W. B. Eerdmans, 1995.

Young, Robin Darling. "Gay Marriage: Reimagining Church History." *First Things* 47 (Nov. 1994): 43-48.

CHAPTER 6

The Classic Christian Exegesis on Romans 1:22-28

Thomas C. Oden

*M*y method is that of classic orthodoxy: appealing to consensual exegetical texts of the earliest Christian centuries that sought to interpret the mind of the believing church prior to its divisions. By classical exegetes, I refer in case to pre-Protestant exegesis of the first millennium in the era of the undivided church. I will be quoting patristic texts to which Catholics, Orthodox, and Protestants of all sorts, including Charismatics and Pentecostals, can appeal. They set forth the earliest layers of interpretation of Paul's teaching.

Homosexuals are not singled out as a uniquely egregious class of sinners. Rather they are viewed as a pivotal illustration of the general history of humanity under the condition of sin. Please note that Paul is speaking not of what today is widely called a homosexual "orientation," but rather of actual homosexual practice; that is, behavior as distinguished from inclination or tendency or predilection or proclivity or attraction or temptation. The distinction between act and temptation allows Christians to understand same-sex temptations in the context of all temptation, sexual and non-sexual. No one is condemned for being tempted, except to the extent that one colludes with the temptation.

My central thesis is: There is indeed a consensual classic Christian teaching of homosexuality that can be demonstrated textually by setting forth the broad consent of the ancient church in the interpretation of those sacred Scriptures upon which Christians generally agree that faith and moral teaching must be grounded.

My intent is simple: All parties who comment on homosexuality focus especially on one text, Romans 1:22-28. It epitomizes both the reasons for homosexuality and its consequences. Hence I will narrow my focus to these seven verses. My task is not to concentrate on recent comment on these ecumenical exegetes, but to let them speak for themselves. I will not approach the question deductively by attempting to define first what the Christian teaching of homosexuality is, and only then to see if that doctrine is found in Scripture or consensual tradition. Rather I will proceed inductively to discern what the earliest Christian exegetes said about the single pivotal Scripture text.

Classical Christian teaching does not appeal to early consensual exegesis on modern democratic or cultural assumptions. Rather, it proceeds on the premise that the whole community of faith is being guided by the Holy Spirit into all truth amid the hazards of history, and that those exegetes most widely remembered and received, whose writings were preserved by the church of both East and West, and read liturgically, are reliable guides to the witness of the Holy Spirit to the truth of the gospel.[1] Merely conveying the views that follow may cause some to regard the conveyor of the message as biased or mean-spirited. I ask only that my plain task be understood as simple and clear, conveying and accurately reporting the classic Christian consensus, without bias.

My modest objective is: To show textually that there is a well-defined classical Christian consensus on homosexuality. Homosexuality does not yield the pleasure expected. It dishonors the body. It increases the alienation between male and female. It is a voluntary activity.

The passage Romans 1:22-28 divides itself naturally into two parts: (1) the foolish and idolatrous exchange of God for creaturely images, and (2) the exchange of natural for unnatural passions. Both parts involve an exchange metaphor: The first is exchanging the true God for gods; the second is exchanging natural for unnatural passions. The first is divisive for the relation of God and humanity. The second is divisive for the relation between men and women, dividing the sexes against each other. Both are voluntary.

The Context of Disordered Passions

The Fall into Idolatry

Paul writes in Romans 1:21: "For although they knew God, they did not honor him as God or give thanks to him, but they became futile in their thinking, and their senseless minds were darkened" (RSV). Within this matrix of people who "knew God," homosexuals are included, but they are not here designated. Augustine notes of those who "knew God": "Notice that Paul does not call them ignorant of the truth, but says that they held the truth wrongly."[2]

Yet precisely those who knew God as God "did not honor him as God." This is the tragic story of all humanity enmeshed in the history of sin. Gennadius of Constantinople stated this point sharply:

> The pagans knew that there was a God, and it is clear that they did not receive judgment because of this. For it was not for want of knowledge that they were condemned, but for their response to their capability of knowing. For each one glorified some supposed 'god' in the sense that whatever he imagined God to be, that he served. Thus they corrupted the whole matter by their peculiar and mistaken ideas. They abandoned God's way of knowing him and preferred their own way, falling into the deepest foolishness, outdoing themselves in their so-called wisdom by adding to their folly, descending even to the worship of reptiles and inanimate objects.[3]

In this way, all humanity, and not homosexuals only, "became futile in their thinking." Ambrosiaster commented on this sense of futility: "Truly this is futility, that knowing the truth they decided to worship something else,[4] which they knew was not true. Hiding from God they worshiped idols. A cloud of error covered their heart."[5] Pelagius further underscored this premise of volition: "Not only did they not know God, they did not want to know him."[6]

How were our minds darkened? Augustine comments: "Therefore they were given over by the Lord to the desires of their own hearts, and did improper things."[7] And in *On Nature and Grace,* he writes: "By the blinding of the heart because of the abandonment by the light of wisdom, they fell more and more into

grievous sins."[8] Thus far nothing has been said by Paul of homosexuality. But into what "grievous sins" are some humans falling
into "more and more"?

The Foolish Exchange

The exchange is set forth in verses 22-23: "Claiming to be wise,
they became fools, and exchanged the glory of the immortal God
for images resembling mortal man or birds or animals or reptiles"
(RSV). Who became fools? Not homosexuals only, but all humanity who exchanged worship of the creation for the Creator. Here is
the succession as analyzed by Chrysostom: "(1) Paul's first charge
against the idolaters was that they missed finding God. (2) His second was that, although they had a wonderful and clear path for
knowing God, they did not walk down it. (3) The third is that they
nevertheless pretended to be wise. (4) The fourth was that not only
did they not find the Supreme Being, but sought to lower God to
the level of devils, stones and wood."[9]

Therefore God Gave Them Up:
Permitting Freedom to
Live with Its Own Consequences

Romans 1:24 says, "Therefore God gave them up in the lusts of
their hearts to impurity, to the dishonoring of their bodies among
themselves." Who are "they"? Not homosexuals in particular, but
the whole history of idolatrous humanity. Theodoret of Cyrhus
says, "By *gave them up (paredōken)* Paul means that God permitted this to happen. He simply abandoned them because they had
fallen into extreme ungodliness."[10]

"God gave them up in the lusts of their hearts to impurity."[11]
Chrysostom stressed that all idolatry is voluntarily willed: That

> God *gave them up* means that he left them alone. . . . God left
> those who were not minded to receive what comes from him, but
> were quick to desert him, even though God had fully done his
> part. After all, he set before them, as a form of teaching, the
> world. He gave them reason, and an understanding capable of
> perceiving what they needed to do. Yet the people of that time did
> not use any of those things in order to come to saving knowledge,

but rather they perverted what they had received into its opposite! What could God have done about this? Could he have forced them to do what was right? Yes, but that would not have made them virtuous. All he could do then was to leave them to their own devices, which is what he did, so that in that way, if in no other, having tried and discovered the things they lusted after, they might turn away from what was so shameful.[12]

They Dishonored *(atimazō)* One Another's Bodies

A century before Chrysostom, Origen had summarized this as an ecumenical consensus:

> This is the faith of the church: For just cause those who, in their wickedness, suppress the truth revealed by God are abandoned by God, and because they are abandoned, they are given over to the desires of their own hearts. The desires of their heart were that they should disgrace their bodies in uncleanness and abuse, and that with corresponding neglect towards the worship of God, they should abandon the glory of the incorruptible God for the wicked and base forms of men and animals, and think so little of themselves as to live like irrational beasts when in fact they were rational men.[13]

Did God cause this or allow it as a result of the exercise of human freedom? God did not protect them from dishonoring their own bodies, but rather respected their freedom to become foolish. The anonymous pietistic commentary on The Holy Letter of St. Paul to the Romans confirms this: "In saying that God gave them up to their own lusts, Paul is not claiming that God is the direct cause of their idolatry. Rather he is saying that God did not bring immediate vengeance on them even after much patience and long-suffering. God simply allowed them to act according to their own desires."[14] So they exchanged the truth about God for a lie, serving the creature, not the Creator. Augustine commented: "By worshiping and serving the creature rather than the Creator they have wished not to be a temple of the one true God."[15] Ambrosiaster wrote: "They damaged each other's bodies with abuse. For even now there are men of this type, who are said to dishonor each other's bodies."[16] The body is damaged and dishonored when put to a use not intended by the Creator.

The Exchange of Natural for Unnatural Passions

What dishonorable passions? Now a major transition occurs in Paul's argument. He illustrates the general principle with a specific example. Romans 1:26 says: "For this reason God gave them up to dishonorable passions. Their women exchanged natural relations for unnatural" (RSV). Here, homosexual practice (they "exchanged natural relations for unnatural"—*metēllaxan ten physiken chrēsin eis ten para physin*) specifically enters for the first time into Paul's discussion, as a dramatic case in point, illustrating the larger human predicament (idolatry).

Ambrosiaster set forth Paul's distinction between what is natural and what is unnatural sexually:

> Paul tells us that these things came about, that a woman should lust after another woman, because God was angry at the human race *because of their idolatry*. Those who interpret this differently do not understand the force of the argument. For what is it to change the use of nature into a use which is contrary to nature, if not to take away the former and adopt the latter, so that the same part of the body should be used by each of the sexes in a way for which it was not intended? Therefore, if this is the part of the body which they think it is, how could they have changed the natural use of it if they had not had this use given to them by nature? This is why he said earlier that they had been handed over to uncleanness.[17]

In this passage, Ambrosiaster is assuming that (a) sexual practice may occur according to its natural use *(physiken chrēsin)* or "contrary to nature" *(para physin)*; (b) each part of the body is given by God for some natural use; (c) if persons freely choose to change the use of nature into a use contrary to nature, such as to use the tongue as a substitute penis, or to use the anal orifice as a substitute vagina, they bring upon themselves the displeasure of God for this voluntary abuse of God's gift of natural sexuality; and (d) the root cause of this displacement is idolatry, lacking respect for the gifts of creation in their intended arrangement. Hence to forget God is to forget the deeper meaning of our sexual nature.

Many distorted human behaviors eventuate out of this idolatry. Paul's list makes it clear that homosexuality is only one of many such behaviors that dishonor God. No sin noted in this detailed catalog is primarily focused on sexuality. He says: "They were filled with every kind of wickedness, evil, covetousness, malice. Full of envy, murder, strife, deceit, craftiness, they are gossips, slanderers, God-haters, insolent, haughty, boastful, inventors of evil, rebellious toward parents, foolish, faithless, heartless, ruthless" (Rom. 1:29-31). Pelagius adds: "Once lust is unbridled, it knows no limit. In the order of nature, those who forgot God did not understand themselves either."[18]

Why Are Lesbians Discussed First?

It is noteworthy that Paul deals first with lesbian homosexuality and only then later with male homosexuality. One might otherwise assume that women would have a more developed sense of shame for the abuse of that which is unnatural, as Chrysostom notes: "How disgraceful it is when *even the women (te gar theleias)* sought after these things, when they ought to have a greater sense of shame than men have."[19] It is no compliment to men that one expects better from women.

The source of pleasure is that which is natural: "Genuine pleasure comes from following what is according to nature. But when God abandons a person to his own devices, then everything is turned upside down."[20] Yet God, by temporarily abandoning the lesbian to her own devices, does not ever give up finally upon her redemption. God continues to pursue her with infinite patience and love: "God gives up on no one. The word is used only when he leaves people to their own devices."[21] To follow one's inclinations against nature does not elicit either pleasure or happiness.

Those who abandon the order of nature abandon the author of nature. Pelagius reasoned: "Those who forsook the author of nature could not keep to the order of nature." "God gave them up to dishonorable passions" (Rom. 1:26 RSV). Hence those "who turned against God turned everything on its head."[22]

They changed a natural function into an unnatural function, according to Tertullian: "When Paul asserts that males and females changed among themselves the natural use of the creature into that which is unnatural, he validates the natural way."[23] The blessings of marriage are affirmed as the "natural way" to honor God through sexuality. Having dealt with lesbian sexuality, Paul now turns to male homosexuality, as an analogous case in point of the idolatry that leads to folly.

And Men Likewise Gave Up Natural Relations with Women

Romans 1:27 says: "And the men likewise gave up natural relations with women and were consumed with passion for one another, men committing shameless acts with men and receiving in their own persons the due penalty for their error" (RSV). When men are consumed with sexual passion for other men, the reason is not merely lust, but idolatry: "It is clear that because they changed the truth of God into a lie, they changed the natural use of sexuality into that use by which they were dishonored." [24]

The arena of these "shameless acts" is "men with men," not men with women. They demean human dignity, according to Cyprian, who regarded "men committing shameless acts with men" as "an indignity even to see," from which one naturally turns one's eyes away. He thought homosexual acts constituted a dishonoring behavior that "a chaste countenance cannot even look at" without being inwardly harmed and demeaned.[25]

This loss is very costly to men. What do they give up? The natural for the unnatural. They give up the special joy provided by the Creator between a man and a woman. They left behind "natural relations with women" *(tēn physiken chrēsin tēs theleias)*. For this reason, men lusting for men receive "in their own persons the due penalty for their error" (Rom. 1:27 RSV). They themselves are responsible not only for their contempt of their own bodies, but also for their contempt of God, says Ambrosiaster: "Paul says that the due penalty comes from contempt of God, and from this comes wickedness and obscenity. For this contempt is the prime cause of sin."[26]

The fathers thought that homosexuality tended to intensify the enmity between men and women. It makes women enemies of men and men enemies of women. The abandonment of the natural complementarity of the sexes, Chrysostom says, stands as "clear proof of the ultimate degree of corruption, when both sexes are abandoned. Both he who was called to be the leader of the woman, and she who was told to become a helpmeet to the man, now behave as enemies to one another."[27]

Homosexuality intensifies the war between the sexes: "The normal desire for sexual intercourse united the sexes to one another; but by taking this away and turning it into something else, the devil divided the sexes from each other, and forced what was one to become two, in opposition to the Law of God." The Adversary "was bent on destroying the human race, not only by preventing them from copulating lawfully, but by stirring them up to war and subversion against each other."[28] The devil prefers to divide the sexes and take away the joy of ordered sexual blessings. "Men with men" appear to outdo even the devil in imagination. The devil is constantly struggling against the natural. What is natural in sexuality is seen between a man and a woman in covenant fidelity looking toward the protection of children.

The Loss of Pleasure in Homosexuality

There is a noted absence of pleasure in male homosexuality. When males are "consumed with passion" for other males, Cyprian wrote, "Men with frenzied lusts rush against men. Things are done which cannot even give pleasure to those who do them."[29] These males are burning in the erotic desire of one male toward another male *(exekauthēsan en tē orexei auton)*, each seeking to use the other for his own immediate gratification, contrary to the long-range purpose and pleasure of sexuality in bonding the sexes and caring for children.

Chrysostom counters the argument that homosexual behavior is a form of love:

> Notice how deliberately Paul measures his words. For he does not say that they were enamored of one another, but that they were consumed by lust for one another! You see that the whole of desire comes from an excess which cannot contain itself within its proper limits. For everything which transgresses God's appointed laws lusts after monstrous things which are not normal.[30]

Homosexuality is most displeasing to itself: "What is contrary to nature has something irritating and displeasing in it, so that they could not even claim to be getting pleasure out of it."[31] This is the displeasure into which God permits homosexuals to descend by the free exercise of their will in order to bring them to new life. The result of idolatry was to drag down both men and women, pitting them against one another. It did not deliver long-term pleasure; it elicited a heightened readiness to tolerate other accelerating evils.

God Gave Them Up: The Willingness to Tolerate Unnaturalness

Romans 1:28 says: "And since they did not see fit to acknowledge God, God gave them up to a base mind and to improper conduct" (RSV). Origen notes: "This is the third time that the Apostle uses the phrase *God gave them up*. Each time he gives reasons for this, but the reasons do not seem to correspond to the causes. . . . It is therefore better to take all three instances together, and regard them as a single cause for the abandonment of men to their lusts." [32]

Sexual toleration invites toleration of other evils, thought Ambrosiaster:

> Because they thought they could get away with it, and that God would look the other way, and were therefore prone to neglect what they were doing, Paul adds here that they were more and more reduced to folly and became ever readier to tolerate all kinds of evils, to the point that they imagined that God would never avenge things which no one doubted were offensive to humanity as well. He now lists all the evils that were added to these, so that if they should be converted to normal reason, they might recognize that these evils befell them because of God's wrath.[33]

The longer train of evils became more easily tolerated because unnatural sexual excesses were tolerated. While toleration is a prototypical modern virtue that defines the limits of all other virtues in a hyperconflicted society, toleration in excess is regarded by the Fathers as a danger to the truth and an obstacle to wisdom. The homosexual life is portrayed as one that nurses the improbable fantasy that God will look the other way. One evil intensifies many evils: covetousness and malice, "from which flows envy, murder, strife and deceit. After this he put malignity, which generates gossip and slander."[34] Many corruptions weaken the will to resist corruption: "Notice how everything here is intensive—*filled* and *with all.* Having named maliciousness in general, Paul goes on to discuss the particulars, and these too he mentions in excess—*full of envy, etc.*"[35]

Why Homosexuality Is Voluntary

Homosexuals are

> responsible for their own sins, and Paul deprives them of all excuse. For he says that their evil deeds did not come from ignorance, but from willful practice. This is why he did not say: *because they did not know God,* but rather: *they did not see fit to acknowledge God.* Their sin was one of a perverted determination of obstinacy, more than of a sudden ravishment, and it was not in the flesh (as some heretics[36] say), but in the mind, to whose wicked lust the sins belonged, and from which the fount of evils flowed. For if the mind becomes undiscerning, everything else is dragged off course and overturned.[37]

Wrote Gennadius of Constantinople: "God is not responsible for destroying anyone. . . . Paul says rather that God went away from them and left them to their own devices, so that their false understanding of God might appear to be the cause of their evil life."[38] Chrysostom says: "No one can say that it was by being prevented from legitimate intercourse that they came to this pass, or that it was from having no means to fulfill their desire that they were driven into this monstrous insanity."[39]

The objection may be made: The context may modify or moderate the meaning of the text. But the Romans letter is notably a teaching letter intended to be circulated to other churches and applied in different contexts. Exhaustive inquiry into context, authorship, social assumptions, and philology does not alter the substantive argument that the Fathers grasped easily, just as any reader can grasp today. Others may object: So what? These are ancient texts, so they can be discounted. That is just the point of this exercise: Ecumenical teaching faithful to the deposit of faith cannot forget or set aside either the pivotal text of Scripture on homosexuality or its consensual interpretation.

My conclusion is: The Fathers understood themselves to have received a well-defined classical consensual Christian teaching on homosexuality. It is grounded in idolatry, not simply lust as such. It dishonors the body. It tends divisively to pit male against female. It does not yield the pleasure expected. It is a voluntary activity. It demeans human sexuality.

CHAPTER 7

The Real Disagreement

Elizabeth Moreau

*P*robably not since slavery has The United Methodist Church witnessed and been party to such vehement and often hostile disagreement akin to the debate over homosexuality. It is arguable that even the ordination of women did not evoke the polarization within The United Methodist Church currently seen both nationally and locally. Perhaps for this reason, or perhaps because of initial similarities, the Church's debate over homosexuality is too frequently couched in the language of civil rights. However, homosexuality is not finally a civil rights issue; and as long as the discussion remains one of civil rights, the deeper and more significant issue at stake cannot be addressed; that is, the role and authority of Scripture within the worshiping community of faith.

Both slavery and the rights and ordination of women were battles fought over the appropriate moral interpretation of the scriptural authority; the disagreement over homosexuality is fundamentally a disagreement about what or how much authority the Scripture is to have in the contemporary Church. Consider, for example, the ambiguity of the biblical witness regarding women: On the one hand, Paul instructs women not to speak, teach, or have authority over a man,[1] although in other passages, Paul encourages women leaders in the early church and holds them up as examples of godliness.[2] Thus, the debate over the equality of women was, at least in significant degree, a debate over apparently contradictory teachings within the primary authority for Christian life: Scripture. The biblical witness regarding slavery is even more ambiguous in that there is no record of Jesus or Paul ever actually addressing the social sin of slavery.

In contrast, the biblical witness is uniform in its rejection of homosexuality, not only in explicit written condemnation, but also in the complete absence of any positive homosexual role model anywhere in the Bible.[3] Unlike past debates linked to civil rights, in which the interpretation and morality of particular biblical passages were in conflict, there is general agreement about what the Bible actually says regarding homosexuality.[4] Therefore, the entire debate surrounding homosexuality focuses on whether that biblical teaching can be normative for this generation of Christians. While the debate over women's rights and slavery arises from within the biblical texts, the second debate over homosexuality challenges the biblical texts themselves.

It is this undermining of the role and authority of Scripture within the Church that has created such an impasse. How we receive and interpret the Bible depends upon how we understand the authority of Scripture. What we must realize is that, should the Scriptures cease to be authoritative for The United Methodist Church, we will cease to be a part of the church, which has existed from the day of Pentecost onward. It has always been the case that the gospel stood outside the culture to which it spoke and judged that culture with the mercy and grace of Christ; it has never been the case that the culture judges the faithful obedience of the church. If the real disagreement underlying the conflict is the question of the applicability and relevance of the ancient writings for today's Christian, how can we understand them to speak to contemporary society?

Although the writings that make up the Bible are predominantly from the first century, it was not until the late fourth century that the writings were compiled into the list, or canon, that comprises today's New Testament.[5] There were a large number of Gospels and letters circulating in the first four centuries, but the early church determined this particular list of books, which now constitute the New Testament, to be authoritative for Christian life and faith.

However, long before there was ever an official biblical canon, the texts that now make up the New Testament were in use within the church. The basis for giving authority to the books of the New Testament was their influence on the lives of individuals as divinely revealed truth. The content of the many ancient writings varied substantially, and those books that accurately depicted the nature of God, human nature, the human condition, and the gift of salvation *as experienced by individuals* converted to Christianity became the primary teaching texts of the church. In the centuries between the times the texts were written and the church canonized the New Testament, these particular writings had already become authoritative within the early church because they functioned as a means of grace through which individuals encountered and came to know the living God in Jesus Christ. The experience of the early church was that through prayerful study of the message contained in these writings—the Gospels and letters we now call the New Testament—lives were transformed by the truth divinely revealed.

Thus, the source of the authority of the Bible is nothing less than divine revelation; God reveals himself to us through these particular writings and, in so doing, reveals to us our own being, nature, and condition. Stating the obvious, there can be no appeal to a higher authority than God. Moreover, the only reasonable construal of creation is to conceive of its existence as an expression of its Creator. Logically, an omnipotent God could have created any imaginable number of cosmoses; however, if a particular god chose to author a particular creation, then that creation is necessarily ordered in a particular way reflective of its creator. All of the components of the story must necessarily cohere in a manner that illuminates, enlightens, and explains its existence, its source, and its meaning, for the story to be recognizable and for it to have transformative power in the lives of individuals. To the extent that the creature/creation reflects the Creator, any change in the order of creation likewise reflects a change in the Creator, that is, to alter one portion of the story necessarily influences another piece of the story; the story ceases to make sense and must be reconceived in a coherent manner.

Furthermore, once we have changed the order of creation—such things as the nature of human relationships, the purposes of human sexuality, and the identity of sin—then these changes must also be reflected in the nature of the Creator. Literally, the God revealed to us must be altered, become a distinctly different god. The reason the debate over homosexuality is so intense is because it brings into question the whole idea of divine revelation. The counterclaim that homosexuality is compatible with Christian teaching challenges the truth of divine revelation: Did God not reveal the truth to us through Scripture? If the Bible is wrong on an issue it specifically addresses, on what issues is the Bible authoritative? What biblical teaching *can* be trusted?[6] It is inevitable that the Bible ceases to function as a means of grace to salvation and is reduced to a series of encouraging stories and helpful suggestions subject to personal preference.

For the generations that followed, the early church proved itself to be guided by the Holy Spirit. The humble study of Scripture has led people to Jesus Christ. As persons subject themselves to scriptural instruction, they receive new life in Christ and are transformed in Christ's image (in Wesleyan language, justified, sanctified, and perfected). Across the span of two millennia of history, through wars, plagues, and the rise and fall of nations, these Scriptures have sufficed to bring salvation to people. Even today, as old and culturally relative as the biblical texts are said to be, this Bible continues to bring new life in Jesus Christ to such culturally diverse churches as the church in Africa, the church in Asia, and elsewhere. Only within Western Protestant Christianity has the notion of improving upon the divine revelation found in Scripture become commonplace.

We are faced with a dilemma at this point. Either the God who is the source of these writings has played a grand, malevolent joke on billions of people who think they have received spectacular grace and salvation but are wrong, *or* these Scriptures are in fact divinely revealed truth whereby we can be saved. After two thousand years and billions of Christian conversions, a measure of humility is in order. To make the counterclaim that homosexuality is compatible with Christian teaching, and thus to receive the Scripture in a manner at odds with the interpretation of every other branch of the church of Jesus Christ, one must depend upon extensive—as well as selective—knowledge from human sources.

The exegetical methods of biblical interpretation used to overcome the biblical teaching on homosexuality arise from contemporary secular philosophy, scholarly proposals committed to reading the Bible without any possibility of divine revelation. Virtually all academic assumptions begin from a secular mind-set, excluding the proposition that God exists, much less speaks.[7] It would seem, then, that for the average Christian to be able to read the Bible and understand what it really means, as opposed to what it merely seems to report, he or she must have highly specialized knowledge in the latest exegetical methods for biblical interpretation. This stands in stark contrast to Article V of the Articles of Religion of the United Methodist *Book of Discipline,* which states that "Holy Scripture containeth all things necessary to salvation."[8]

Perhaps more significant is this approach to biblical interpretation that implies a sort of modern-day gnosticism, in which secret or special knowledge is required to understand the Scriptures and, therefore, to encounter and know God. If we take seriously the notion of human sin, then we finally cannot allow human knowledge and experience to judge divine revelation; rather, divine revelation judges human knowledge and experience. The role of Scripture is to take the human experiences of sin, darkness, and death, and through the light of revelation, bring human beings to the fullness of life in Jesus Christ, to true freedom as sons and daughters of God.

Through humble, prayerful study, the teachings found in the Bible call us forth from darkness to light, from bondage to freedom, from death to life. This has been the experience of Christians throughout the history of the church and across the globe today, that these Scriptures reveal the pathway to salvation by bringing persons to the transforming knowledge and love of God in Christ Jesus. Realistically, homosexuality is a relatively minor issue in Scripture. Unquestionably, the Christian church can and should be in ministry with and to the homosexual community. It is not a question of whom the church will baptize or to whom the church will offer the Sacraments, but rather a question of what gospel will be preached.

If it is necessary to abandon the authoritative teaching of the Bible, then we have little to offer the homosexual community, and everyone else for that matter. When we dismiss the Bible's portrayal of sin, we must also discard the promises of new life and transformation found in the Bible. To alter our understanding of the human condition, we must be prepared to change the nature of God, the nature of salvation, and on and on. All of these concepts are inextricably linked in one cohesive and coherent story in the Scriptures. If we now abandon the gospel of the Scriptures to accommodate cultural preferences, then we do not have the gospel of Jesus Christ, at least not a gospel recognizable to the great cloud of witnesses who have gone before us.

In short, changing The United Methodist Church's position on homosexuality is like pulling a thread, which then unravels the entire fabric. The end result is, if salvific truth for this generation cannot be found in the Bible, it will be necessary to establish those contemporary writings that do have greater authority than Scripture and that do provide the means of grace for human beings, whether that be the *New England Journal of Medicine*, the *Journal of the American Psychiatric Association*, *The New York Times*, *Reader's Digest*, *Good Housekeeping*, or any other writing deemed to convey the truth necessary for our salvation. Our other option, of course, is to commit ourselves to the belief that nothing exists in our lives from which we need to be saved—a commitment of folly, for sure. However, that assumption is the driving force behind efforts to change the Church's position on homosexuality.

Because some persons feel a compelling urge for homosexual relations, the urge itself must be a natural inclination, thus wholly good and given by none other than God himself. By the same logic, virtually every sin that occurs in human life turns out not to be sinful. Human beings sin because we cannot think of anything better to do; we sin because sin is *natural* to us.[9] The ancient Scriptures teach that the human condition is one of sin, and the vast majority of us experience the destructive reality of our sinfulness with great clarity on any given day. Tragically, there are few more measurably destructive behaviors—physically, psychologically and spiritually— than homosexuality. Only blind determination can hold to the conviction that one's natural inclinations are wholly good. It is ironic that this propensity for self-destruction is exactly how the Scriptures depict human nature, and it is from precisely this inclination and inevitability that we all must be saved. Scripture stands like a massive, immovable rock; we either cling to it in hope of salvation or run into it full speed ahead and bounce off in misery, claiming "there's nothing there."

The identity of the church throughout the ages has been built upon the writings found in Scripture. When the Bible we have ceases to be authoritative for our denomination, then we have to realize we have broken continuity with the historic church and the proclamation passed down through the ages. Although it seems highly unlikely, it is conceivable that we have found new truth greater than the gospel proclaimed by Christians everywhere for all time; but when we change the gospel, the Good News, then we have changed religions. We can dress this other new truth up and call it Christianity, but no one from the second century, the eighth century, the fifteenth century, and no one from the churches of Africa or Asia would agree.

Although the debate within The United Methodist Church has focused almost exclusively on homosexuality, the far more serious underlying issue is the authority of Scripture, and it is this issue that must surface if we are ever to understand the full ramifications of the conflict in our denomination. The following quote from the senior pastor of a reconciling congregation makes abundantly clear the depth of the chasm between the two views of the authority of Scripture:

> Now it is our turn to get honest. Although the creeds of our denomination pay lip service to the idea that Scripture is "authoritative" and "sufficient for faith and practice," many of us have moved far beyond that notion in our own theological thinking. We are only deceiving ourselves—and lying to our evangelical brothers and sisters—when we deny the shift we have made. . . . We have moved far beyond the idea that the Bible is exclusively normative and literally authoritative for our faith. To my thinking, that is good! What is bad is that we have tried to con ourselves and others by saying, "We haven't changed our position."[10]

What is at stake in the debate over homosexuality is what one believes Jesus Christ has to offer homosexual individuals, indeed all individuals. Either we are going to offer the gospel as revealed to us in Scripture, or we are going to offer a gospel of our own making, something that is already happening in far too many of our pulpits. That is why the debate is so ferocious and the conflict so relentless. The issue is not merely homosexuality; homosexuality is the starting point for a debate over the content of the Christian faith.

PART III: THEOLOGY

CHAPTER 8

The Creation/Covenant Design for Marriage and Sexuality

Maxie D. Dunnam

*B*iblical/Kingdom community is established on the idea of covenant. Covenant faithfulness is expressed in the context of relationships. Succinctly put, biblical community founded on covenant faithfulness in the context of relationships is bound up in the sacrificial love of God and neighbor. Jesus instructed us that the Kingdom community is not defined by marriage or singleness or even traditional notions of family, but rather by all who do the will of God. While our community is not defined by these social conventions, it is exclusively made up of them. It behooves us to examine our unique source of revelation, the Bible, as it relates to marriage and singleness and family in order to understand the context out of which we labor to do the will of God. Particularly, for purposes of this essay, we examine the nature and purposes of the gift of human sexuality and its expression in ways that build and do not destroy community and maintain faithfulness to the revealed idea of covenant faithfulness.

Even if the Bible made no references to homosexual acts, the biblical view of marriage would exclude them. When we reflect on the biblical witness, especially our Lord's teaching on marriage, we are confronted with the will of God. When we center on God's will and

God's revelation for humankind, Jesus' teaching has to be placed front and center in our deliberations. Thus, we must begin with the doctrine of creation, which makes sex holy in the biblical sense. Life is holy because it belongs to God. A vessel or a sacrifice is holy when set apart for God. So sex is a gift from God, a holy gift that cannot be separated from the human body, mind, and spirit; thus, it is to be used for knowing and glorifying God. The strongest case for the Church's position against homosexual acts, the blessing of same-sex unions, and the ordination of practicing homosexuals, is the doctrine of creation and the biblical affirmation of heterosexual marriage. Clues of God's intention for humanity are present in the creation story (Gen. 1 and 2).

> So God created humankind in his image,
> in the image of God he created them;
> male and female he created them.

God blessed them, and God said to them, "Be fruitful and multiply, and fill the earth and subdue it; and have dominion over the fish of the sea and over the birds of the air and over every living thing that moves upon the earth." (Gen. 1:27-28)

Then the LORD God said, "It is not good that the man should be alone; I will make him a helper as his partner." (Gen. 2:18)

Then the man said,

> "This at last is bone of my bones
> and flesh of my flesh;
> this one shall be called Woman,
> for out of Man this one was taken."

Therefore a man leaves his father and his mother and clings to his wife, and they become one flesh. (Gen. 2:23-24)

The description of marriage is placed in the biblical narrative of creation with all that is pronounced *good* by God prior to the rebellion and the Fall. Four constituent aspects of marriage are indicated. One, it is an exclusive union between two persons; it is singular—"a man." Two, it is a community or social affair: "leave his father and mother." Three, it is a loving, caring covenant, which is heterosexual and permanent; the man "clings" to his wife. Four, marriage is consummated in sexual intercourse between man and woman; the two become one flesh.

Creation and Marriage

Though the author of Genesis was not consciously or specifically prohibiting same-sex relationships, the relationship of marriage described here is consistent with commands about sexuality throughout the Bible. The biblical account of creation, which suggests the model of Christian marriage—one man, one woman in a lifelong monogamous relationship—should be a strong enough argument against homosexual practice.

The thread of covenant marriage is celebrated by both Jesus and Paul:

> Some Pharisees came to him, and to test him they asked, "Is it lawful for a man to divorce his wife for any cause?" He answered, "Have you not read that the one who made them at the beginning 'made them male and female,' and said, 'For this reason a man shall leave his father and mother and be joined to his wife, and the two shall become one flesh'? So they are no longer two, but one flesh. Therefore what God has joined together, let no one separate." They said to him, "Why then did Moses command us to give a certificate of dismissal and to divorce her?" He said to them, "It was because you were so hard-hearted that Moses allowed you to divorce your wives, but from the beginning it was not so." (Matt. 19:3-8)

> "All things are lawful for me," but not all things are beneficial. "All things are lawful for me," but I will not be dominated by anything. "Food is meant for the stomach and the stomach for food," and God will destroy both one and the other. The body is meant not for fornication but for the Lord, and the Lord for the body. And God raised the Lord and will also raise us by his power. Do you not know that your bodies are members of Christ? Should I therefore take the members of Christ and make them members of a prostitute? Never! Do you not know that whoever is united to a prostitute becomes one body with her? For it is said, "The two shall be one flesh." But anyone united to the Lord becomes one spirit with him. Shun fornication! Every sin that a person commits is outside the body; but the fornicator sins

against the body itself. Or do you not know that your body is a temple of the Holy Spirit within you, which you have from God, and that you are not your own? For you were bought with a price; therefore glorify God in your body. (1 Cor. 6:12-20)

Marriage is a lifelong commitment, which involves the bonding of two persons, male and female, in mutual love and commitment. The only vehicle able to contain the gift of human sexuality is covenantal marriage.

A careful reader of the creation story can't miss three references to "flesh." "This is flesh of my flesh"; "they will become one flesh." This is not a casual, nondeliberate account, but a clear picture of God creating male and female for each other. Their sexual differences and the coming together of those differences express God's intention and commands. "So God created humankind in his image . . . male and female . . . blessed them and said, 'Be fruitful and multiply.'"

We admit with joy that the sexual relationship involves everything that makes us male and female and is far more than reproduction. Even so, God's design for creation is the continuation of humankind through the shared reproductive sexual relationship of man and woman. It is not unreasonable to say that since homosexual union cannot produce children, therefore it is "unnatural," both in the biblical and biological sense.

Some may raise the question about couples unable to have children. The fact that there is a deep sadness when such occurs is a witness to childbearing being a part of God's design for marriage. A couple's inability to conceive is painful and not to be seen as God's will, but as unfairness of life. That we wrestle with the question, "Where is God in this?" comes out of the pervasive human awareness of God's intention for a man and a woman to be joined together in love and "be fruitful."

Complementarity in God's Creation of Male and Female

Add to this line of thought the notion of complementarity in God's creation of male and female. There is ongoing debate among scholars about whether differences between male and female— social roles, ways of thinking, and so on—are present at birth or are learned behavior. Whatever the cause, it is obvious that there are marked gender differences, and these are deeply ingrained. The Genesis story affirms the difference—in fact presents it as a part of God's plan—and makes the point that the union of the two—male and female—constitutes completion. In terms of sexual differences, physical complementarity is undoubtedly present. The way God has created us makes sexual intercourse between male and female "natural." The female vagina is made to receive the male penis; the anus is not.

Though reasonable and derived from Scripture, physical complementarity is only a part of the case for Christian marriage. Sexual complementarity is more than the act of sexual intercourse, and the notion of complementarity is deeper than reproduction. Heterosexual partners in marriage not only bond as they "fit" physically together in corresponding body parts, but also become "one" as they open themselves and respond to the mystery of the other gender. They honor God and each other by surrendering their bodies to the design of God—to their reproductive capacity and also to male-female complementarity. The complementarity of male and female sexual organs provides a symbol at the physical level of the much deeper spiritual complementarity. Again, Paul chooses the Genesis language to reflect on the mystery of marriage, even going so far as to use it as a metaphor for Christ's relationship to the church: "'For this reason a man will leave his father and mother and be joined to his wife, and the two will become one flesh.' This is a great mystery, and I am applying it to Christ and the Church" (Eph. 5:31-32).

We noted earlier that both Jesus and Paul endorsed the creation narrative definition of marriage. Focus again on Jesus. He introduced his discussion of marriage by quoting Genesis 1:27 that the creator "made them male and female." He concluded with his own comment, "so they are no longer two, but one flesh. Therefore what God has joined together, let no one separate" (Matt. 19:6).

This comment of Jesus was in response to a question about divorce:

> He thus made three statements about God the Creator's activity. First, God "made" them male and female. Secondly, God "said" that a man must leave his parents and cleave to his wife. Thirdly, he "joined" them together in such a way that no human being

might put them apart. Here, then, are three truths which Jesus affirmed:

1. Heterosexual gender is a divine creation;
2. heterosexual marriage is a divine institution; and
3. heterosexual fidelity is the divine intention.

A homosexual liaison is a breach of all three of these divine purposes.[1]

Responsibility: Personal and Community

Thomas E. Schmidt reminds us that *responsibility* is a part of male/female complementarity and must be a key factor in the way we honor God as sexual beings:

> Heterosexual union is good because only it can produce children and because only it joins in partnership two fully complementary people. Children are . . . a consequence of heterosexual union; and the production of children is good because it involves parents in another level of love, that is, the gift and nurture of a new and dependent life. The [nurturing] of children by their parents is good because it allows children to learn from both sexes and especially to find a model in the same-sex parent for the development of their own sexuality.[2]

Responsibility is not only an individual issue, but also a community one. Those within the church who champion the cause of homosexual practice always include two arguments: One, these persons are *made this way*, so how can we deny them the right to express who they are. The second argument flows from this one: "What right do I have to defy or impose normative sexual practice? What harm can come from consenting adults gratifying themselves sexually?"

That persons are *made this way* is not a settled fact. There are no scientific studies that provide irrefutable evidence that homosexuality is genetic. The cause question is a very complex one: To what degree is homosexuality or any behavioral trait genetic or nongenetic, affected by or independent of environment, biological or sociological, familial or nonfamilial, innate or acquired? Perhaps the most responsible conclusion is that both *nature* (genetic) and *nurture* (familial and societal conditioning) make us "who we are."

Explanations of the "way we are" do not provide justification for "how we act." What may seem *natural* and "feel good" in human expression or human desire may, in fact, violate God's *natural* moral design. This is the reason the Church, throughout our history, has taken the position that the practice of homosexuality is a violation of God's *natural* moral design and undermines God's intention for family. The big push by homosexual activists within the Church today is to approve long-term adult relationships of mutual consent. This is a call to something that in the history of human cultures no society has ever approved. The appeal to the unproven theory that "it's *natural*" ("that's just the way I am") is to seek a radical individual freedom that is irresponsible to community: "it's what satisfies me."

The Church must keep perspective on this issue. The affirmation of homosexual practice is ultimately destructive of family, which is the foundation of society. We must pay attention to the architects of the homosexual rights movement. It is not enough to "follow our hearts" and feel sympathetic for those we know and love who either by nature or by nurture respond to their homosexual inclinations and passions. We see the larger picture and the cultural/sexual revolution that is not only ripping the fabric of our church unity, but also is destructive of the family as the common good of society as we know it.

To keep perspective, the Church must stay aware of the radical agenda of the homosexual cultural and political lobbyists. Listen to Marshall Kirk and Hunter Madsden as they quote Michael Swift, a homosexual activist: "The family unit—spawning ground of lies, betrayals, mediocrity, hypocrisy and violence will be abolished. The family unit, which only dampens imagination and curbs free will, must be eliminated."[3] Kirk and Madsden consider Swift typical of gay media radicals and suggest that homosexuals tone down such rubric in order to pursue a "mainstreaming" strategy.[4] So, activists who write for the wider public, and those within our Church who plead for "inclusion of homosexual brothers and sisters in the church," do tone down their language and couch their advocacy primarily in civil rights and Christian acceptance language in order to bring homosexuality into the cultural mainstream. The fact remains: We are in a sexual revolution, and behind what seems to

110

be the championing of civil rights and bringing the Church into harmony with the cultural tide of fashionable notions is a fallout that is destructive to human wholeness and violates God's intention for family and the Kingdom community.

We must be clear that this has to do with not only homosexual practice, but also every sexual relationship and activity that deviates from God's revealed intention—polygamy, cohabitation, adultery, serial marriages, casual and temporary sexual liaisons. All are equally displeasing to God and are under God's judgment.

When we read the more sophisticated advocates of homosexual liberation, we see the inherent conflict, even war, between homosexuality and heterosexuality. Unless we have clarity at this point, we will continue to think somewhat superficially about the issue. Unless the Church speaks clearly, the media's presentation of homosexuality as though it were culturally acceptable and normative will shape our attitudes and responses, and there will be ongoing confusion about responsibility.

Schmidt observes that an interesting example of this confusion is the 1993 film *Philadelphia,* the story of a homosexual man dying of AIDS and whose employer fires him when his condition is discovered:

> In one of the key scenes the hero and his lover visit the hero's big family home in the country, where his half-dozen married siblings and his parents sit in a circle and without exception express support for the hero's lawsuit and (indirectly) his homosexuality. The mother even says, "I didn't raise my kids to sit in the back of the bus," drawing an obvious parallel between her son's case and the civil rights movement. The rather heavy-handed moral here is that families should offer this kind of unanimous and unqualified support to their homosexual members.
>
> But it strikes me as odd that this kind of support must come from the hero's biological family . . . rather than from the homosexual community. If the message of homosexual liberation is that heterosexual fidelity, childbearing and family nurture are not necessary to human fulfillment, why does the hero need to go *there* of all places to find strength for the coming crisis? Everything about the scene screams tradition—except the explicit message. One comes away with the suspicion that this family is being used by a person whose lifestyle symbolizes its negation.[5]

Leaving many plot questions unresolved, the film resorts to a favorable jury verdict, prompting Schmidt to ask if this is "only Hollywood, or has sympathy become the measure of justice."[6]

The media prevails in its influence, shaping the minds and morals of modern culture, and the church too often surrenders to the tide. The media, moral relativists, and biblical revisionists join in seeking to make the principle of self-fulfillment the rule of life. We are told that to disallow any person to chart an individual course of personal satisfaction in any area of life, including sexuality, is to repress and oppress.

What about Jesus' call to deny ourselves? At the very center of Christian discipleship is our participation in the death and resurrection of Jesus. The call to follow in the way of the cross involves various forms of self-denial:

> So ultimately it is a crisis of faith: Whom shall we believe? God or the world? Shall we submit to the lordship of Jesus, or succumb to the pressures of prevailing culture? The true "orientation" of Christians is not what we are by constitution (hormones), but what we are by choice (heart, mind, and will).[7]

The Witness of Scripture

Let me return to the theme of God's intention in creation and witness of Scripture. The Church's stance against the practice of homosexuality is clearly supported by God's Word. The Reformation and Wesleyan principle, "Scripture should be interpreted by Scripture," prevails. The New Testament use of the Genesis passage of God's creation holds the most significance. The teachings of Jesus on divorce and marriage are found in Matthew 19:4-8 and Mark 10:6-8. The Mark passage begins with the words, "But from the beginning of creation, God made them male and fem ale," and then quotes Genesis 2:24-25: "Therefore a man leaves his father and his mother and clings to his wife, and they become one flesh. And the man and his wife were both naked, and were not ashamed." It is unmistakably clear that Jesus interprets the passage to mean there is a sacred order of sexes that is grounded in creation itself, expresses God's will for humankind—heterosexual, monogamous marriage—and provides the only context for sexual intercourse.

In 1 Corinthians 6:13-20, Paul quotes only verse 16: "The two shall be one flesh"; but in Ephesians 5:25-33, he repeats the entire verse of Genesis 2:24. As David Seamands reminds us,

> In both instances he *spiritualizes* the one-fleshness, that of heterosexual intercourse to describe the believer's union with Christ as being "members of Christ" (1 Cor. 6:15) and joined to His body. In Corinthians, Paul uses it *negatively* to condemn fornication as a misuse of the body which is "not your own" (v. 19). In Ephesians he uses it *positively* as a symbolic analogy of Christ's love for the Church. In both instances the sacred heterosexual order of creation is made the basis for moral imperatives.[8]

Those who espouse homosexual rights and oppose the Church's stance on homosexual practice argue that there are other issues about which the Church has changed its position to other than that which is stated in Scripture. The primary issues that they raise in that regard are slavery and the place of women within the Christian church. There are, admittedly, ethical issues in Scripture (slavery and the place of women are among those), in which specific moral directives vary according to the cultural and sociological context of the biblical times. With these two issues (slavery and the role of women in the Christian church), there is a *trajectory*, or track, in Scripture that, linked with our understanding of the mind and spirit of Jesus, leads us to know that slavery and oppression of women is contrary to God's will.

In matters of sexual morality, there is no question: One common thread runs throughout all Scripture, and it never varies. It is a clear and consistent: God's design in creation calls for the honoring of heterosexual marriage. From that, the *trajectory* makes it clear that heterosexual relationships are God's design, and the practice of homosexuality violates that design. As Christians, we must connect our ethic and theology of sexuality with our theology and ethic of marriage. In God's order of creation, marriage is good and blessed. In marriage, we have a metaphor for God's love of God's people, as shown in Hosea's pursuit of his adulterous and promiscuous wife, Gomer (Hos. 1–3). Paul says explicitly in Ephesians

113

5:25-33 that marriage, in the relationship of husband and wife, is to reflect the mystery of Christ's love of his bride, the church.

Summary

The marriage of one man and one woman in an everlasting covenant is not an incidental human notion; it is a creational reality. It is abundantly clear that sexual intercourse is to be reserved for that relationship of marriage. Christian Scripture consistently condemns all other forms of intercourse: fornication, adultery, incest, and bestiality. Along with that, homosexuality is always condemned as being outside God's creative order—and incompatible with God's intention for us, his children. When the Bible addresses same-sex intercourse, it is always clear, unambiguous, unequivocally, and unanimously negative. But again, the discussion and debate is best served by focusing on the larger issue of revelation and God's created order. When we reflect on the biblical witness, especially the creation narratives and Jesus' teaching on marriage, it is clear that God's will is heterosexual marriage—one man and one woman in a lifelong monogamous relationship.

CHAPTER 9

Contentious Conversations

Myths in the Homosexuality Debate

Joy Moore

*D*uring the last third of the twentieth century, The United Methodist Church, along with a number of other denominations, has engaged in contentious debates concerning the issue of homosexuality. Encountering pressure from a shifting society, some groups from within the Church advocate the recognition of homosexuality as an optional lifestyle. In spite of successive legislative action maintaining the Church's restrictions against homosexual practice, those opposing the position of The United Methodist Church[1] continue to campaign for tolerance and full acceptance of persons who engage in homosexual activity. Defenders on both sides of the issue too often resort to name-calling, simplistic scriptural solutions, and fear induced political tactics.

For the community called Christian, the challenge to intersect real issues with a biblically guided life is necessary. Many are reluctant to continue in a dialogue when the principles expressed are so polemical, establishing positions rather than engaging in shared dialogue. One voice speaks for contemporary culture, only to receive a response of religious orthodoxy. Another voice, seeking a theological discussion, hears political argument. Nonetheless, conversations matter if community is to be preserved.

This chapter will consider some of the arguments rehearsed by those who wish to move the Church to a new position on homosexual practice. I will attempt to show that these arguments are in fact myths or rationalizations that have emerged during the contest of words in contentious conversations.

Ten Percent Participation Mandates a Change in Moral Standards

A July 2001 column in *US News & World Report* by John Leo reported a significant increase in same-sex households in the 2000 census.[2] Leo qualified the reporting with specific numbers. The census calculations number 250,679 same-sex households, one half of 1 percent of all U.S. households—a significant increase from one tenth of 1 percent in the 1990 census. In 1993, a research arm of Planned Parenthood published a study of 3,321 men. Their findings reported 2.3 percent having had a same-sex experience in the past decade, with 1.1 percent self-describing as exclusively homosexual in orientation. Additional studies find "five to six percent of sexually active adults reported being exclusively homosexual or bisexual since the age of eighteen."[3]

Why are such numbers significant? Alfred C. Kinsey, an Indiana University zoologist, conducted twelve thousand individual interviews, providing an estimate that 10 percent of males and less than 5 percent of females are homosexual for at least three years during their lives. For half a century, Kinsey's 10 percent figure has been widely used, but surveys have not validated this figure. Numerical statistics prove that persons who identify with this practice exist. Accounts of homosexuality are historically chronicled. The biblical record acknowledges a diversity of sexual practices, including homosexuality.

The question is not prevalence, but prudence.[4] Allowing numbers to establish the validity of a behavior begs the question. Homosexual practice has always existed. At issue is not the existence of homosexual practice, but what standards of morality exist for the community called to biblical holiness. Neither polls nor political votes name categories of sin. The identification of behaviors by 2 percent, or even 10 percent, of the population is no reason to change moral standards. Alternative expressions, against which Christian behavior will appear countercultural, will always exist. Even if the culture at large is changing, Christianity is not mandated to alter its identity such that it can no longer be distinguished from the larger society.

Homosexual Behavior Is Not Sin

To allow for this alternative understanding, categories of sin have been redefined. Traditionally, "sin" referred to a rebellious spirit, intentional insubordination resulting in separation from God the Creator; humanity; and, for all intended purposes, creation itself.[5] In contrast, pro-homosexual advocates view the church's greatest sin as its refusal to accept those who are different. They oppose any form of oppression that denies homosexual persons the freedom to pursue relationships of their own choosing. This view holds that homosexual practice merely represents an alternative lifestyle, not a biblical transgression. The Church is asked to do more than allow for alternative practice; Pro-homosexual activists desire affirmation, not just understanding and leniency.

These issues provoke deeper consideration of how far values must shift as sin is redefined. These practices are relevant to this conversation because as homosexual practices are adopted, efforts increase to accept other forms of sexuality, as well as to lower the age of consent. Advocacy for changing standards of sexually permissive activities abounds. Consider that while the American Psychiatric Association presently recognizes transvestite behavior diagnostically as a disorder, some who cross-dress or self-identify more with the opposite gender desire tolerance and approval from society in general. Similarly, the question of bisexuality alters concepts of monogamous relationships. The North American Man-Boy Love Association (NAMBLA) actively promotes homosexual pedophilia as an acceptable alternative form of sexuality. Although the vast majority of those who practice homosexuality would never entertain these types of thoughts, they seemingly allow a vocal minority to dominate the conversation.[6]

It is important to understand persons of homosexual orientation are not, no more than heterosexually oriented persons, exclusively attracted to children. Nor are all transvestites homosexual. Pedophilia, a topic all too often raised in conversations on sexuality, provides an example of the inconsistency in the arguments. To approach such tolerance in contemporary society would require a change in laws, morality, and prejudices. However, this very same expectation of society is made regarding homosexual practice.

Challenged to Hospitality Rather Than Holiness

Decrying the sharply moralistic concerns of most opponents, the application of a human rights approach redirects the dialogue from ethics to hospitality. Those who redefine sin as discrimination are puzzled at the categorical dismissal of persons that they feel are born different. Focusing on vicious antihomosexual behavior, homosexual advocates are able to eclipse the concerns of morality by highlighting human and civil rights. The moral argument disappears in a shift to civility, concentrating on the human right to justice and freedom.

The effort to change moral definitions misinterprets the struggle of past human rights movements. Past coalitions sought to restore full humanity to persons of non-European descent (then viewed as less than human) a century after the elimination of the institution of slavery in America. They requested, not to change ethical standards, but to practice them. For example, the question of interracial marriage was not based on differing values or inconsistent understandings about marriage and sex. The definition of marriage as the uniting of a man and a woman was not changed.

Today's arguments related to same-sex union seek to redefine institutions and change moral categories. To bestow rights of marriage to domestic partners creates a new moral standard. Allowing homosexual unions redefines marriage.

Revising moral standards changes the very ethics that call into question judging a person by birth rather than by behavior. Persons of non-European descent have requested they not be assumed incapable of behaving within the moral and cultural standards of society. Advocates for homosexual practice appeal for a change in cultural mores that will accept particular behaviors traditionally deemed immoral. The former seeks to be allowed to behave within existing ethics, the latter seeks identification by practices presently outside of cultural standards. This is a very different request for rights.

Unlike discrimination against women or persons of color, societal inclinations to censure homosexuals have been a response to behavior, not being. Statistically, self-described homosexuals are counted among persons most affluent, well educated, and privileged. With their higher-education achievements, they are prominent in almost every business and profession. A homosexual lobby influences the media and the political arena. Despite their small percentage of the population, an organized lobby for homosexuals has succeeded in conferring particular privileges and benefits to a category of persons whose claim to distinction is their sexual attraction and behavior. This is not a representation of a deprived class of people. More important, the Church has affirmed the "sacred worth" of homosexuals as children of God.[7]

Homosexuality Is an Immutable Genetic Predisposition

Defining a person by sexual persuasion provides nothing comparable to gender and race. Most people of color have fought against the idea that desires and abilities are defined by Darwinian social stereotypes that suggest one's genetic code establishes ones values and morality. Although studies have been conducted to demonstrate that homosexual orientation is a genetically based immutable characteristic, the American Psychiatric Association maintains that no replicated scientific study supports any specific biological cause or condition for homosexual orientation.

The description of homosexuality as a genetic condition crashes in the face of efforts of civil rights advocacy, arguing against behavior solely dependent on biology. Many persons have recognized their orientation to same-sex eroticism is something they have freedom of choice to act upon. It should be noted that some do, in fact, choose a heterosexual alternative.

The greater part of scientific evidence supports that homosexual orientation is an acquired habit. Major professional mental health organizations have affirmed since 1973 that homosexuality is not a mental disorder. By 1998, the American Psychiatric Association had expressed opposition to reparative treatment based on the negative effects of the presumption that homosexuality is a mental disorder. The assumption of mental illness has caused extensive harm for those struggling with their sexual identification, regardless of whether they view the practice as sinful. For some, that possibility of change offers hope, not only of changing one's sexuality, but also of controlling societal anger, fear, and prejudice. If homosexuality is not a mental illness, it is a habit—like almost all human proclivities.

Homosexuality as an Alternative Lifestyle Is a Christian Option

Concentrating on homosexuality as an alternative lifestyle, pro-homosexual lobbyists argue that identity exists in one's erotic preferences. Ignoring personhood capable of self-control and change, this perspective identifies itself fundamentally with sexuality.

Embracing sexuality as definitive in no way spares one from being human. Biblically speaking, each person must choose to accept or reject the invitation of the Creator-Covenant God to join a community whose ethics and expressions are so distinctive that the world takes note to understand why. The Wesleyan understanding of both human free will and the transformative power of the Holy Spirit stands fundamentally against a predestination to homosexual activity.

Hope and support for *choice* is the sole option of a Church that believes in the power of transformation. It has never been the position of religious tradition that sin represents a *mental* deviance. Rather, the biblical witness assumes human propensity to question authority and advance lifestyles that celebrate individualistic self-satisfaction. Psychology and sociology are sciences that observe behavior, and only Christianity reveals humanity's God-given capacity for alternative choosing. The covenanted obligation of the people of God has always been to be noticeably different from the prevailing culture. Where the God of Scripture is acknowledged and followed, behavior changes. At all cost, Christianity is a divinely ordered holiness, which distinguishes the people of God from others.

Expressions of gay politics have infiltrated the Church as if her agenda were to reclassify subgroups within the Christian community and honor their individual stories. Such chronicling overshadows and minimizes the missional focus of the Church to invite the world to the Creator-Covenant God who retells all humanity into one story. To choose identification by class, gender, or race for others, or for oneself, narrates others out of the story. Such classification rescinds the community-expanding identity of the people of

God, a community formed by its characteristic worship and behavior, reflecting the image of a holy God.

The transformation attested to in the biblical narrative is to be replicated in the lives of those who claim the text as authoritative. Without such transformation of attitude, practice, and belief, the text is reduced to optional tips and techniques. Scriptural authority rests in the divine purpose of God in human history. Such revelation is not evidenced by society's redefinition of sexual identity, but by the transformation of people's fundamental commitments, dispositions, and identities. Such obviously distinctive lives bear witness to the choice of a representative people who acknowledge a world-altering God.

Biblical Passages Regarding Homosexuality Are Ambiguous

Few biblical passages refer to the practice of homosexuality. But each passage has been interpreted to describe this practice as contrary to God's intention for those called to a lifestyle of holiness. Those seeking to change assumptions of human sexuality hold that ancient cultures had little or no understanding of sexual orientation and practice that could result in loving, monogamous same-sex relationships. Therefore, the apparently negative references are not applicable to current discussions. Such limited interpretation does not negate that the Genesis to Revelation narrative, as interpreted throughout the whole of Jewish-Christian history, affirms that sexual intercourse is to be enjoyed within a covenant of marriage between a man and a woman.

For any response to be explicitly Christian, it must acknowledge and respect the scripturally formed community and its tradition. Who we are as Christians is not represented within a single denomination, but in the shared understanding and identity of the church universal expressed ecumenically over the past two thousand years. When deciding Christian options, we must accept both the call to holiness that distinguishes the people of God and the work of the Holy Spirit that reverses human propensity to sin. Eventually, we all must agree a consensus can (or cannot) be reached within our given community. At some point, contentious conversations must again give way to honest conversation.

PART IV: SOCIAL SCIENCE

CHAPTER 10

Homosexuality in the Postmodern World

H. Newton Malony

This essay includes comments on four matters: (1) the changes in attitudes among psychologists and psychiatrists that have resulted in homosexuality no longer being considered a mental illness, (2) the research evidence that homosexuality may have a biological/physiological foundation, (3) the attempt to understand sexuality as a habit formed though life experience, and (4) the description of the homosexual lifestyle that should be troubling to all. As a trained clinical psychologist and ordained United Methodist clergyperson, I feel uniquely qualified to address these matters. These thoughts are intended to contribute to the "Reason" component within the United Methodist *Quadrilateral*.

Changes in Attitudes Toward Homosexuality

I begin with a widely agreed upon definition of "homosexuality" as "erotic attraction toward persons of the same gender."[1] Surveys report that although these kinds of feelings are common at one time or another in many persons' life experience, exclusive feelings of same-gender erotic attraction leading to identifying oneself as gay or lesbian is found in 4 to 5 percent of the male and less than 1 percent of the female population.[2] Although this makes homosexuality quite exceptional and different from the norm, the

American Psychiatric and Psychological Associations have now judged the condition not to be evidence of a mental illness.[3]

A generally accepted understanding of "mental illness" is as follows: Persons who are mentally ill are (1) a danger to themselves, (2) a danger to others, or (3) gravely disabled. Although mental health professionals considered homosexuality to be a mental illness throughout three fourths of the twentieth century, most would agree today that homosexuals, as a group, do not meet the aforementioned criteria. Homosexuals can be found among most professional groups and at every class level of the public. Although it is true that the unprotected practice of sodomy has tended to spread the AIDS virus, the incidence of predatory behavior among homosexuals is the exception and, certainly, is not nearly the threat to society that is associated with heterosexual rape.

However, it should be said that the aforementioned criteria for mental illness are *minimal,* and the basis of disapproving statements made by religious groups, such as The United Methodist Church, stem from a different criterion than simply adjustment to society. The Judeo-Christian tradition has always stood in judgment over any and all culture.[4] Amos, the eighth-century prophet, is a clear example; as the economy of that time was burgeoning, Amos declared social relations between rich and poor to be unjust from a theological point of view. Justice always has to do with safeguarding the rights of minorities. In regard to homosexuality, some have said that justice is the point and society has stepped in when religion has failed because of religion's negative attitudes. It has been said that religion has not protected the rights of gays and lesbians. In fact, this may have been true at times. When religious persons have participated in discrimination, prejudice, and acts of violence, injustice has been done. Christians should never deny the rights or fail to protect the safety of those with whom they disagree.

However, it is one thing to hold the opinion that homosexuality is not the ideal will of God for humans and quite another to say that holding such a view provokes violence against homosexuality. Only the most bigoted human beings would tolerate violence such as, for example, the murder of Matthew Shepherd. It is a travesty, however, that a popular morning news anchor, as well as many liberal Christians, should contend that conservative Christian opinions about homosexuality had anything to do with Shepherd's murder. It is also curious that the same outcry has not been made about the explicitly violent lyrics of the pop star Eminem—lyrics that definitely encourage hatred and harm to homosexuals. Political correctness seems to make it acceptable to criticize conservative Christians but tolerate outlandish behavior from rock stars who influence more youth than the church.

Declaring homosexual behavior as incompatible with Christian teaching, as The United Methodist Church has done, is not the same thing as acting unjustly, discriminating against homosexuals, or participating in violence. There are many socially acceptable behaviors incompatible with a Christian lifestyle, and all believers should persistently examine themselves for areas that they can bring their lives more in harmony with God's will. Here religion reserves the right to declare wrong what society may judge to be correct. Christian ethics and social ethics may not always be the same. In fact, often they are not. It should be remembered that, from a Christian point of view, homosexuality is only one among many areas of life incompatible with Christian teaching.

And what makes homosexuality incompatible with Christian teaching at the same time that homosexuality does not meet the criteria for being called a mental illness? Other chapters in this book discuss the biblical and theological foundations for this assertion in more detail,[5] but suffice it to say that any behavior not in accord with the will of God, as understood in Scripture, experience, reason, and tradition, is incompatible with Christian teaching. In contrast to the viewpoint that conceives homosexuality as a good gift of creation to be celebrated and practiced, the Christian church has traditionally understood homosexuality as sinful—that is, not how God intended people to behave. It is fallen creation, not good creation. As John Wesley contended, Christians are to be busy restoring the creation to its God-intended state, not accepting everything that is, as good.

And what is the "God-intended state" regarding sexuality that traditionally has been affirmed by Christians worldwide? The United Methodist Church has stated it as "fidelity in marriage, celibacy in singleness." Celibacy, not sexual intimacy, is the ideal for all unmarried Christians, heterosexual as well as homosexual, according to this teaching. This does not mean that deep, abiding, even covenanted friendships cannot develop among Christians of the same gender. In fact, Christian teaching encourages such friendships. It would call the motives in such relationships "philos" (brotherly, sisterly), even "agapic" (sacrificial, committed), love. But Christian teachings would exclude "erotic" or sexually intimate love from these relationships. Ideally, from a Christian point of view, in these same-gender or not-yet-married-opposite-gender relationships, it is not God's will that two bodies become joined in the most intimate physical act known to human beings.[6] It is sad that genuine, committed, long-term, nonsexual friendships are sometimes confused with homosexuality in postmodern society.

This teaching about the "God-intended state" for sexual or erotic expression denies neither that sexuality is a God-given gift nor that sexual release is one of the most powerful urges for human beings. But it does affirm, along with Plato, Jesus, and Augustine, that pleasure can never be a primary virtue. Pleasure must serve a higher good, namely, God's will for life. As far as heterosexuality goes, one major denomination affirms this teaching through the motto "True love waits"—a motto to which its youth are encouraged to pledge themselves. True love waits to express sexual intimacy in heterosexual marriage. It matters little what the majority does or what society approves; if young persons follow God's will for life, they will wait until they are married to have intercourse and will remain faithful to one person for a lifetime. To some, this may sound constrictive and naïve, but it remains the teaching of the church. The Christian faith has affirmed this ideal for many centuries and across many cultures. I have no doubt that it will continue to do so.

In regard to homosexuals, the ideal of celibacy is difficult because it proscribes sexual intimacy, but it is not different from the celibacy prescribed for unmarried single persons—a group estimated to be over 6 percent of the population, a percentage greater than that of homosexuals. One person asked me, "Would this teaching not condemn homosexuals to a lifetime of sexual continence?" And the answer is yes. From an ideal, Christian point of view, this is the burden of homosexuality. But it is also the burden of unmarried heterosexuals. Since, at this time in history, United Methodists do not consider holy unions as *marriages*, homosexuals cannot marry. This is not the end of the world, as many *heterosexuals* who do not marry would report. But it is a burden to bear for the sake of the ideal of doing what God wills. Those who contend that exceptions should be made for homosexuals appear to elevate pleasure to a level above doing God's will. While this may be understandable, it is not Christian, from my point of view. Making such an exception for homosexuals also borders on sentimentality devoid of conviction.

The Biological Basis of Homosexuality

The most recent survey of the literature on the issue of whether homosexuality is a biological disorder is contained in the volume *My Genes Made Me Do It* by Neil and Briar Whitehead.[7] Even though the authors note that certain maladies are directly caused by genetic mutation (less than 1 percent), the incidence of homosexuality (2 to 5 percent in the population) is too high to be considered among them. Homosexuality is much more similar to such psychosocial disorders as manic depression, psychosomaticism, sociopathy, obsessive-compulsive disorder, and personality disorders.[8] Whereas genetic disorders result in fixed conditions (as in Down syndrome, phenylketonuria, and Rett syndrome), homosexuality is not a static condition; it changes over time and shows a steady decline as people age. Also, in those disorders that hover between 5 and 10 percent in incidence, most persons engage in considerable efforts to control or change the symptoms.

However, it is oversimplistic to assume that questions pertaining to the physiological basis of homosexuality are explained away simply by suggesting homosexuality is not due to genetic mutation. Everyone admits that sexual-identity formation is a developmental process that takes place over time,[9] and this process may well be in part determined by biological predispositions.[10] Certainly, since the Kinsey investigations at mid-twentieth century, a number of scholars have become convinced that the primary basis of sexual attraction is biological rather than psychosocial. Psychiatrist Jeffrey Satinover concluded that this point of view has resulted in three opinions: (1) as a matter of biology, homosexuality is an innate, genetically determined aspect of the human body; (2) as a matter of psychology, homosexuality is irreversible and, where it is forced, results in a denial of self that causes psychopathology; and (3) as a matter of sociology, homosexuality is normal, akin to other categories such as gender and ethnicity.[11]

In an earlier publication, I discussed these three issues.[12] An extensive quotation from this discussion follows:

The *biological* studies have been of three kinds: twin studies, brain studies, and hormonal studies. The *twin* studies have dealt with the question of whether there is such a thing as a "homosexual gene." In monozygotic (identical) twins, sexual orientation should be the same regardless of whether or not the twins were reared apart. However, studies reveal only a 52% rate of similarity compared to 22% for fraternal (nonidentical) twins and 9% for siblings. There does seem to be a biological component in homosexuality but it cannot be attributed to a "homosexual gene"—else the similarity rate would be 100%. How significant is this component and whether it is absolutely determinative of behavior is not known at present.

Brain studies have focused on the finding that autopsy examinations of homosexual and heterosexual men found differences in both the volume and number of cells in two areas of the brain. Assuming that sexual orientation and behavior were the only features that distinguished these two groups, an assumption that was hard to confirm since all the men were dead, the question still remains whether correlation means causation. It is well known, from other non-sexual studies, that life experience can change the development of certain cranial features. In the case of these studies, there is no way of knowing whether homosexuality caused the cell development, or the cell development caused the homosexuality. In all fairness, however, there is some theorizing that in gestation, femaleness is the default condition and that homosexuality is a deviation from that state. It could be that the development of the hypothalamus in males, where at least one of these studies reports differences, is along a continuum. It is possible that the development of the hypothalamus deviates significantly less in homosexual males than it does in heterosexuals.

Hormonal theories have focused on the prenatal process and the times at which certain types of neurological organization appear and develop. Noting that some homosexuals differ significantly in overt mannerisms from heterosexuals, theorists have proposed that traumas, chemical ingesting, and/or hormonal imbalances may have occurred at specific prenatal periods. There have been no studies of these theories to date although the general theory that unusual prenatal, embryonic experiences are significant for later functioning is widely accepted.[13]

The *psychological* issue has been whether sexual orientation is a changeable feature of personality or not. Since the 1971 decision of the American Psychiatric Association and the 1973 decision of the American Psychological Association to officially desist from labeling "homosexuality" a mental disorder, there have been considerable pressures on both these organizations to declare "reparative therapy," counseling directed toward changing sexual orientation, unethical. This pressure has been based on the yet-to-be proven presumptions that homosexuality is a genetic predisposition over which persons have no control.

The evidence [does] not support such a conclusion and neither of the APAs have voted to outlaw counseling to alter sexual orientation or behavior. . . . [The *APA Monitor*] reports the decision of the American Psychological Association . . . to permit such counseling . . . when done with great care and when it is requested. . . .[14] While such a decision clearly distinguishes between ego "dystonic" and ego "syntonic" homosexuality, it clouds the fact that those for whom their homosexuality is no longer a problem, the syntonic group, may have reached that state by massive denial and social conformity.[15]

It is paradoxical that at the May, 2001 meeting of the American Psychiatric Association, psychiatrist Robert L. Spitzer of Columbia University, who had been at the forefront of the APA's decision in 1973 to no longer judge homosexuality to be a mental illness, reported that over 65 percent of 200 ex-gay and lesbians persons he studied attested to good heterosexual functioning. His conclusion was that "some gays can change"—not only their behavior but, also, their orientation. Of particular interest for our discussion is the fact that Spitzer's subjects were predominantly Christians who ascribed their change to the transforming power of God.[16]

Homosexuality as a Habit Problem

In my opinion as a psychologist, *all* sexual behavior is habitual. This is true of heterosexual as well as homosexual behavior. Habits are those interactions with the environment that people repeat again and again in order to predict outcomes that perpetuate survival and provide satisfaction. Philosophers have called these motivations to survive and find satisfaction "life's vital forces." Although research has not demonstrated that sexual orientation is totally biological, it is true that both the drives toward survival and pleasure (satisfaction) are givens in human life. In this sense, both are essential or physiological. They are normal. If this is what is meant by saying "sex is a gift from God," then I agree.

To develop this theme a bit further, it is also true that while heterosexual behavior often results in offspring, the dominant motive behind almost all sexual behavior is *satisfaction* or *pleasure—not survival*. Sexual behavior, regardless of whether heterosexual or homosexual, does not extend personal survival. Engaging in sexual behavior is what people do after their survival has been assured.

The question remains, *Why is it that there is no culture, ancient or modern, in which homosexuality is the norm?* Here I think we do have to bring physiology into the conversation. The bodily structure and function of males and females seems fitted for heterosexual forms of sexual behavior. It is not incidental that anal intercourse among gay men often results in disease. There is a sense in which heterosexuality is "doing what comes naturally." "Nature" seems to have favored heterosexuality. Homosexuality has always been atypical.

Psychologists would, therefore, see homosexuality as a *habit problem*. Homosexuality, both as orientation and as behavior, is understood to have come about through distorted interactions with the environment. While not true in every case, research has shown a decided relationship between childhood sexual abuse and adult homosexuality. This relationship holds true even when the experience was not seen as unpleasant for the child. Further, Western culture has too often engaged in the kind of gender stereotyping that provoked some male youth who had interests in the music and the arts and female youth who had interests in sports and science to have confused self-concepts. While many theorists have gone beyond the psychoanalytic thesis that strong parents of the opposite sex paired with weak parents of the same sex provoked homosexuality, it is still a truism that home environments are crucial in the development of sexual identity. Some lesbianism clearly has been provoked by abusive heterosexual relationships. Again, American culture's emphasis on physical appearance has, at times, left some men and women devoid of the typical experiences of dating and romance. Further, stereotyping has made it difficult, at times, for high-achieving women to engage in satisfying heterosexual relationships. While no one of these descriptions fits every situation, enough of them have merit not to ignore the fact that some homosexuality has an unfortunate personal history behind it.

Homosexuals must function in a world in which their condition is the exception, not the rule. They are indeed "sexually challenged"—today's politically correct term for what used to be called "sexually handicapped." But their *condition* does not warrant rejection to any degree. As The United Methodist Church has stated, "Homosexuals are persons of sacred worth," and, as such, they are to be accorded compassion, concern, support, and the grace of God.[17] Neither their orientation nor their behavior is to be viewed, however, as necessarily exemplifying what God intended for human life.

Christians make a clear distinction between feelings and behavior. Homosexual *feelings* do not automatically lead to homosexual *behavior*. While Christians do not see homosexual *feelings* as God's will, they recognize that the Scriptures only disavow the validity of homosexual *behavior*. It is not that the Bible is ignorant of sexual "orientation" (that is, feelings, impulses), as some have contended. In fact, in one of his most severe teachings (Matt. 5:27-28), Jesus states that persons who looked on other persons with lustful feelings have committed the sexual act already. This could apply to homosexual as well as to heterosexual persons. Persons are to control their feelings in order to live up to high ideals they have chosen for themselves.

In this sense, sexual *behavior* is always chosen. Sexual impulses can be acted upon or resisted. This is a truism, but one that needs to be made because sometimes homosexuals claim that they cannot help themselves. We do not allow heterosexuals to make such claims. We penalize heterosexuals if they force themselves on another person, and we expect a certain bit of decorum and faithfulness in marriage. Sexual *behavior* is always voluntary. That is why we have the ruling in United Methodism that we will not ordain "self-avowed, *practicing* homosexuals."[18] Persons can identify themselves as homosexuals and still be ordained if they do not *practice* homosexuality. And we have some ministers who are nonpracticing homosexuals. I have counseled them. They have been successful in channeling their feelings in other ways than acting out. We assume a person does not have to act on every impulse they have. Incidentally, The United Methodist Church would not ordain self-avowed, practicing *heterosexuals* who were being promiscuous or unfaithful. It has always puzzled me why bisexuals are frequently included with homosexuals as those we should accept without judgment since to engage in sexual intimacy with one gender at one time and another gender at another is, by definition, a chosen action.

Of prime importance in this discussion of habits is the assertion that "what is learned can be unlearned." This is the psychological maxim underlying the Christian promise of salvation and transformation (see 2 Cor. 5:17 about the "new creation"). Change of such deep-seated, long-standing, habitual sexual impulses is slow, at best, and often extremely difficult. But psychologists and Christians have hope for homosexuals just as they have hope for those who suffer from many other maladies.

Homosexual Lifestyle

Earlier I noted that homosexuals as a group did not meet the criteria for mental illness. However, there are some troublesome features of their lifestyles that merit attention. Since Christians consider the body as the temple of the Holy Spirit (1 Cor. 6.19), they should be concerned about behaviors that endanger their health or compromise their ability to be of service to others. Psychiatrist Jeffrey Satinover reports a number of these dangers that have been associated with homosexuality in his book *Homosexuality and the Politics of Truth*. He noted that the likelihood of heterosexual males contracting AIDS was 7 in 10,000 but that epidemiologists estimate the rate for homosexual males to be over 300 in 10,000. Thus, homosexuals are over four hundred times greater risks than heterosexuals for contracting this life-threatening illness. Satinover attributes this astounding fact to the larger number of sexual partners and the involvement of the anus in sexual intimacy—this last often being connected to rectal cancer and other infectious diseases.[19]

Another astounding fact is that while homosexuals compose less than 5 percent of the population, they account for 80 percent of all sexually transmitted diseases. The rate of their contracting such diseases is two hundred times greater than among heterosexuals. Lesbians tend to contract syphilis nineteen times more often than their heterosexual counterparts. The figure for gay men contracting syphilis is fourteen times greater than for heterosexual men.[20] Lesbians are six times more likely to be substance abusers than heterosexual women.[21]

Longevity is another area in which homosexuality has been a determining factor. A 1991–92 survey of newspapers available to homosexual communities found that among homosexuals not suffering from AIDS, the median age of death for 5,371 persons to be 42 years of age, with only 9 percent living to old age. Among lesbians, the average age at death was 45 years. Both these figures are dramatically below the life expectancy of the population in general.[22] A well-known fact is that there is a much higher rate of suicide among homosexuals.[23]

Psychologist Joseph Nicolosi reported an in-depth study of 156 homosexual couples.[24] Two thirds of the couples had entered the relationship with the explicit expectation of sexual fidelity. Only seven couples had achieved that goal. Of those seven, no couple had been together over five years. Of course, there is the societal fact that "marriages" have been denied homosexuals, but one wonders whether change in the law would have significantly affected this statistic.

Also, a well-known fact is that the gay and lesbian community has been insisting on public acceptance of their lifestyle. They have encouraged schools to set up clubs for gays and lesbians, and they have had workshops to train teachers in nondiscriminatory teaching. It is unfortunate that their zeal has tended to overwhelm their social judgment, as can be seen in a recent workshop on homosexuality in Massachusetts. The workshop was attended by teachers and children as young as twelve years of age. It was led by gay workers from the state board of education. The program included training in "queer sex" and "fisting" (both so identified in the printed program). Among the speakers were those who presented homosexuality as a normal alternative to heterosexuality and advocated complete approval of all kinds of sexual intimacy. Although the state board of education sponsored the workshop, the public outcry over the event was so great that the leaders lost their jobs.

This workshop exemplified the extremes to which the gay and lesbian community were willing to go to assert themselves. While they would find much support for justice and basic rights, there is also a feeling that they have gone too far and that the health and morality of their lifestyle does not support the level of privilege they are demanding.

Conclusion

This essay has attempted to provide support for the assertions of The United Methodist Church regarding homosexuality by lifting up concerns related to modern social-behavioral science. In this, the twenty-first postmodern century, these conclusions about the ways attitudes toward homosexuality have changed, the evidence for a physiological basis, the nature of habit formation, and the consequence of the gay and lesbian lifestyle would seem important to consider when Christians make their decisions about homosexuality. In my opinion as a clinical psychologist, The United Methodist Church has been on solid ground in asserting that homosexuality is not compatible with Christian teaching. I state this in spite of the fact that homosexuality does not meet the criteria for being labeled a mental illness.

Further, there is no firm evidence that homosexuals are born that way. While there may be biological predispositions in some cases, homosexuality in general is best considered a psychosocial condition, in which the distinction between *orientation* and *behavior* will remain important. Behavior is chosen even when impulses feel compelling. In all cases, homosexuality is a learned habit, and in many cases, homosexuality becomes an addiction. Finally, while not a mental illness, homosexuality is socially atypical and physically unhealthy. At best, homosexuals are "sexually challenged" but are entitled to justice and nondiscrimination.

Most important is that Christians have the right, and the obligation, to look at life through the eyes of the will of God and to call persons to live up to the high ideal of transforming a fallen creation. The conclusions I have drawn in this essay are intended to lend support to the *reason* dimension of quadrilateral thinking, which is thought, by many, to be the foundational model for United Methodist thinking.

References

Allen, J. E. "Health Agenda Focuses Attention on Gay's Needs," *The Los Angeles Times*, 30 April 2001, sec. S. pp. 1, 5.

———. *Perspectives on Homosexuality: The Transforming Point of View*. Pasadena, Calif.: Integration Press, 1998.

Byne, W., and B. Parsons. Human sexual orientation: The biological theories reappraised. *Archives of General Psychiatry 50* (March 1993), 228-39.

Hill, J. R., Jr. "Homosexuality and Health." In *Perspectives on Homosexuality,* pp. 36-38.

Malony, H. "Reason and Homosexuality." In *Perspectives on Homosexuality,* pp. 8-10.

Nicolosi, J. *Reparative Therapy for Male Homosexuality: A New Clinical Approach.* Nothvale, N.J.: Jason Aronson, 1991.

Niebuhr. H. Richard. *Christ and Culture.* New York: Harper, 1956.

Owen, W. F., Jr. "Sexually Transmitted Diseases and Traumatic Problems in Homosexual Men." *Annuals of Internal Medicine 92* (1980): 805.

Satinover, J. *Homosexuality and the Politics of Truth.* Grand Rapids, Mich.: Baker Book House, 1996.

Sleek, S. "Resolution Raises Concerns About Conversion Therapy." *The Monitor of the American Psychological Association* (October 1997): 15.

Whited, R. M. *Redirecting sexual orientation.* Ph.D. diss., The Graduate School of Psychology, Fuller Theological Seminary, 1992.

Whitehead, N. and B. Whitehead. *My Genes Made Me Do It: A Scientific Look at Sexual Orientation.* Lafayette, La.: Huntington House Publishers, 1999.

CHAPTER 11

Marriage

One Man, One Woman

Richard A. Hunt

As we examine The United Methodist Church's position on
marriage more carefully, we must first bow in deep confession that
we as a denomination and as leaders have sinned against God and
God's original creation of marriage. For many decades, we have
ignored, glossed over, trivialized marriage, and ignored biblical and
theological foundations for marriage.[1] Jesus says in Mark 10:2-12
that God's original intention is for man and woman to join each
other as equals in marriage for life, with no divorce.

The issues of same-sex unions and of abortion hold all of us
hostage and keep us from focusing on solutions to the more urgent
problems that arise out of dysfunctional families. We need better
education and preparation for marriage, parenting, and family living. In our Church, we have made such an idolatry out of individual rights that we have failed to sustain support for healthy
marriage. Demands for accepting same-sex "unions" as marriage
have produced deep divisions among us because we have lost sight
of the deeper significance of marriage.

Leaders have been fearful of offending divorced persons, couples
who live together in a sexual relationship without the vows of marriage, persons involved in extramarital affairs, persons with sexual
addictions, as well as homosexuals. Although we affirm that pastors are "to perform the marriage ceremony after due counsel with
the parties involved,"[2] the nearest we have to a Churchwide program for doing this is the *Growing Love in Christian Marriage*

135

books. Often pastors and leaders have failed to do the challenging work of providing adequate pre-wedding counseling and education of engaged couples and failed to follow up couples after their weddings with continuing nurture and support. Into this void, gay and lesbian supporters have brought the heresy of same-sex covenants as equal to man-woman marriage.

In our Church's social principles on the nurturing community is stated that sexual relations are to be clearly affirmed only in the marriage bond.[3] The United Methodist Church has made commendable efforts to emphasize man and woman as completely equal in our UMC service of marriage.[4] "The covenant of marriage was established by God, who created us male and female for each other";[5] "Holy matrimony, which is an honorable estate, instituted of God, and signifying unto us the mystical union that exists between Christ and his Church."[6]

Marriage is at heart a "man-woman" question, the basic special way in which man and woman are invited to understand and love each other across their lifetime journey. "The intimate personal relationship of a man and a woman as husband and wife has served as the principal paradigm for understanding how men and women should be related in all of life. . . . Since God created Man male and female, both must acknowledge the call of God to live creatively in a relationship of mutual trust and confidence, learning through experiment in relationship what God has ordained that they should learn in no other way . . . that in love and humility they may together fulfill their common destiny as Man."[7]

Too often in practice we have implied that "traditional marriage" is an unequal patriarchal relationship, thus failing to support persons in the difficult and challenging lifework of creating true intimacy and communion as wife and husband before God and the world. We have opened the door to the current heresy that gender does not matter in marriage, and therefore, a same-sex sexual relationship can be idealized as a "holy union." This has allowed even the term "holy union" to be stolen from its original application to marriage and forced us to clarify constantly that marriage means "one woman, one man" as co-equal spouses in marriage.

The ecumenical foundation for Wesleyan convictions are plainly and persuasively displayed in four ways: scriptural, theological, experiential, rational, which is the Wesleyan quadrilateral.

Scriptural

Marriage between man and woman is lifted up as a positive part of God's creation (Gen. 1:26-31; 2:15–4:26). God's powerful general covenant (Exod. 19, 32:1–34:15; Deut. 29–31) gives us power to live faithfully in marriage, family, and community relationships. God's call to this "special covenant of marriage" continues even when humans fail.[8]

In Hosea 1–3, marriage is a metaphor of the covenant between God and Israel. Adultery is seen as a sin against both God and neighbors. Always this condemnation is accompanied with an invitation to restoration. Because of Hosea's own painful experience, he can feel some of God's sorrow over the sinfulness of God's people; Hosea's loyal love for Gomer is a reflection of God's concerns for Israel; God wants to heal them, but they continue with hardness of heart to rebel (Hosea 4–14). Out of Hosea's deep understanding of both marriage and its dysfunctions, including adultery and divorce, marriage becomes a metaphor for betrayal and for God's covenantal love (Judg. 2:17).

The experience of woman and man in marriage also serves as a metaphor for the kingdom of God (Matt. 25:1-13; Luke 14:16-24; Rev. 19:7-10). Jesus' clear affirmation of marriage as the God-given crucible by which man and woman come to know and love each other (Mark 10:2-12) does not allow for divorce or any other escape from the tough work of growing in love for each other.

The equality of woman and man is clearly affirmed in 1 Corinthians 7. According to many scholars, the often quoted Ephesians 5:22-32 affirms both wife and husband as "submitting" themselves and their marriage to God, not as a hierarchical superiority of man over woman.[9]

Theological

The word "marriage" comes from *maritus*, as "conjugal," and from *maritare*, meaning "to wed," which in turn means "to bind together, to unite, to blend." The Old English "weddian" is "to pledge" or "to bet." As a contraction "we'd" can mean "we should," "we could," or "we would."

Having both sexes present in marriage gives equal access to each other and ways for man and woman to know each other fully, to learn both to give and to receive, with equal opportunity to talk and to listen in true intimacy.[10]

Bailey traces the shifts in purposes of marriage and family from Old Testament times. He reminds us that Augustine emphasized the blessings of marriage as "'offspring' (which included not only the begetting and bearing of the child, but its being 'lovingly welcomed, kindly nourished, religiously brought up'); 'faith,' or fidelity to the partner in marriage; and 'sacrament,' or the signification of the union."[11] Bushnell also described the nurture of children as a major expression of Christian faith.[12] Bailey prefers to emphasize heterosexual "sex as a gift of God, and marriage as a vocation," also an emphasis of many since.[13] "God has laid upon us all, by making Man male and female, the unconditional task of living in sexual partnership. . . . We are created for each other and bound together by a tie of mutual dependence."[14]

Historically the primary purposes of marriage have been described as mutual love, procreation, and social order.

Mutual love, bonding, and support are so that both wife and husband give and receive care. Marriage is an "awe-inspiring mystery" that calls both sexes to equal regard, tests commitments, examines vision, deepens quality of love and care, and challenges ways we do things. Our experience of marriage becomes the basis for understanding God's covenant love for us (Jer. 31:31-34) and God as a "cosmic lover."[15]

Procreation and socialization of child into society are not just conception and biological birth, but also being stable enough to parent the child (a minor) until she or he "comes of age" to maturity (eighteen or twenty-one years old today). The need to assign responsibility for the conception and parenting of children was a major factor in making marriage a public institution.[16]

Social ordering of sexual drives intends to assure that all are safe from unwanted sexual advances from anyone, male or female, so that no one manipulates another person into sexual activities even when the recipient acquiesces due to threats, pressures, fear, or blackmail.

Allen emphasizes companionship and procreation as the two primary purposes (or goods) of marriage as a "special covenant," based on his explanation of the "inclusive covenant" that guides human society and ethics.[17] Christians see "marriage [as] the norm for intimate man-woman relationships. . . . Judgments about other kinds of intimate man-woman relationships—about unmarried couples, extramarital liaisons, premarital intercourse, group marriages, and all the rest—depend upon and reflect judgments about marriage, whether intentionally or unintentionally." Only marriage between one woman and one man can provide the possibility for equal regard companionship between that woman and that man.[18]

Healthy heterosexual equal-regard marriages are the context in which man and woman can equally know each other and demonstrate for their children the deep awe-inspiring covenant love originally envisioned by God in creation. This is the calling or vocation of both wife and husband.[19]

Experiential

Our current struggles around "holy unions" and marriage can serve the common good of challenging us to deeper modern understandings of marriage as one of the major ways we prepare ourselves to understand God as "cosmic lover" with at least as much passion, energy, and intensity as we humans experience as "lovers" in healthy marital sexuality. It is as if God says to humans, "You want to know what real creativity, dependability, and intense love are? Then how about being creative, intense, consistent, and faithful in living together in marriage, which is both a very private affair and a totally public affair? Then you will know what God is like as Creator, both of the farthest, most awesome creation of galaxies as well as the intricate arrangement of the atoms that form the cells of your body."

Add to this the challenge of children: "You want to know what it is like to be God? Okay, try being parents to a few children, with all the struggles of sibling rivalries, respect for property and person, and so on, that are normal parts of every family, and then come back to see how God feels about parenting a whole world (some six billion "children").

We must be clear that the "one woman, one man marriage" we advocate is not in any way a return to a "traditional" or "authoritarian" (whether patriarchal or matriarchal) marriage. Marriage continues to be a work in progress, as it has been for centuries. Thanks to many sources, including advocates for women and for homosexuals, today we increasingly see marriage as the God-given crucible in which man and woman meet and "know" each other (in the full biblical meanings of sexual intercourse and procreation, as well as all the other subtle contrasts between woman and man). The easy answer would be to assign each gender specific roles in marriage, but this is inadequate because it diminishes the freedom, flexibility, and creativity of both man and woman, both in marriage and in society. The more difficult challenge is for both woman and man to hold each other in "equal regard" in all matters, seek to give loving care as well as receive it, and share power knowing that neither has a majority vote. Absolute co-equality before God releases both man and woman to the fullness of creativity, joy, awe, and mystery in all aspects of marriage.

Rational

"Rights are . . . always social rather than individualistic matters."[20] Equal rights and responsibilities require both sexes to be in marriage as the opportunity for woman and man to give each other equal regard, beginning at home and extending into all of society.

The question of "rights," such as "women's rights" or "gay and lesbian rights," too often implies that a certain class of persons has more "rights" than other groups. If the term "men's rights" is used, it usually implies some type of male superiority or control. We seldom if ever hear of the corresponding "straight rights." Every person's "rights" are limited by the "rights" of all others. All persons are entitled to the same rights and are to be held accountable for the same responsibilities.

Marriage and the Homosexual Lobby

Rather than take up the difficult challenge of learning how to be male with female or female with male in marriage, Nelson counsels too easy an acceptance of the homosexual lifestyle and a diminishing of the values of marriage and other heterosexual relationships.[21] We can welcome his emphases on co-equal human relationships yet strongly assert that God did indeed create two sexes, two genders, as part of the continuing process of creation.

In effect, the homosexual lobby seems to be saying that if the woman/man marriage advocates will not accept same-sex unions as a "marriage" then the homosexual advocates will attempt to disrupt both marriage and the church order (witness the confrontations at the 2000 United Methodist General Conference). This is the reverse of what same-sex "marriage" advocates accuse "straight" advocates of doing when they stand for one man, one woman marriage.

Lifting up woman/man marriage as the only acceptable relationship for sexual activities is not "heterosexism" or "homophobia." The parallel can also be said: That the calls by advocates for homosexual "equal rights" and "gay/lesbian/bisexual rights" amount to "homosexism" and "heterophobia."

Sex is not an idol. To identify oneself as gay, lesbian, bisexual, or straight puts one's focus on sex, not on self in relation to God. It also issues a warning to those in the category as potential targets for the satisfaction of sexual desires. Among heterosexuals, some may erroneously assume that all men want only one thing (sex) from any woman, and that all women want only one thing (money) from any man. Persons are more than the label or category.

Identifying oneself by a sexual label is equivalent to identifying oneself primarily as a member of a political party (Democrat, Republican, Independent, and so on). To fight for the "rights" of gays, lesbians, or straights is to place one group against another. We are all human beings created by God and as such have equal responsibilities as well as "rights" to care for one another.

Homosexual orientation arises from the complex interactions between one's environmental experiences in relation to genotype and phenotype characteristics. Science does not yet have very accurate measures of how gene combinations are related to sexual plumbing, desire, orientation, number of sexual partners, and preferred sexual activities. We do not have sufficiently precise measures to be able to know measures, what actually happened to and influenced persons when growing up.[22]

We all are challenged to discipline ourselves and make decisions that give equal regard to both men and women, to self and to family and society. A same-sex couple cannot and does not give equal regard to the other sex, else each person would have chosen to be in a man/woman marriage. Although genetics and socialization are factors in sexuality, we cannot use these as excuses for current decisions and behaviors.

Caring, however, does not mean giving the demanders whatever they are asking. If a child throws a tantrum to get something, the wise parent does not give in to the child's demands. Sometimes love means having to say you cannot do something (such as touch the pretty flame, drive while intoxicated, abuse someone else, and so on).

The current controversies about marriage, fostered primarily by the homosexual lobby and their sympathizers, are reminiscent of the controversy in the 1800s over bigamy. In 1862, the U.S. Congress first passed a series of laws to prohibit polygamy. After some twenty-five years of conflict, the federal definition of marriage as one man and one woman was finally firmly established in 1887 when the U.S. Supreme Court declared the Reynolds-Tucker Act constitutional.[23] This clear definition of marriage was compromised in 1996 when Congress decided that the definition of marriage is to be left up to each state. In this vacuum over thirty states have passed some type of law declaring that legally sanctioned marriage consists of one man and one woman, and more states are working toward this goal.

Toward a Synthesis and Solution

There are at least four major personal dimensions of marriage:

1. Spiritual—between identity of persons and God.
2. Spouse and family networks.
3. Society/state—what structure/order in society best accomplishes the most good for society.
4. Church—As the incarnation of God, the body of Christ in the world.

At the most inward spiritual level there are many commitments that persons make to others, including being a parent or child, caring for relatives and friends, giving to one's community, and being citizens. We already have services that bless these types of commitments without seeking to make them equivalent to marriage, which they cannot be.

However, marriage is additionally a matter of ordering relationships in families, society, and the church. At ordination in The United Methodist Church, both Deacon and Elder are asked to affirm that they know the "General Rules of our Church" and will keep them.[24] The General Rules call us all to do no harm, do all the good we can, and participate in the ordinances (such as public worship, ministries, Lord's Supper, family and private prayer, and searching the Scriptures) of God.[25] Seek to understand more completely these dimensions of covenant faith and order. Paragraph 331.1(I) of the *Discipline* asks pastors to decide whether to marry a couple (officiate at weddings). Years ago, it was assumed that there could be an "innocent party" in divorce, but today, most family system perspectives affirm that both spouses contributed to the marriage or divorce outcome. Article 21 (Par. 62) describes the "nurturing community" yet needs deeper understanding of the unique significance of marriage as the central relationship in family life.

The standards for ordination in The United Methodist Church "call for higher standards of self-discipline and habit formation in all personal and social relationships."[26] We call upon all Christians, especially United Methodists, to keep the standards we have without circumventing them through euphemisms such as "holy union" in order to justify homosexual couples as "married."

We are all challenged to keep the high standards to which we are called—"fidelity in marriage, celibacy in singleness." God requires tough discipline of us all. Although homosexuals may complain that they cannot, or will not, seek to grow beyond their homosexual desires, so heterosexuals may complain that staying sexually exclusive and faithful to one person is far too much to ask, or that serial monogamy is a much easier and kinder solution than being challenged to work out one's own sexual and spiritual salvation with the person with whom one vowed to journey through life.

At the societal level, marriage is fundamentally about culture's stake in its future, how children are socialized and raised, the basic way to organize the procreation of children and require man and woman to take responsibility for the children they cause to enter the world. Society must structure who is to be responsible for infants, just as society must make decisions about how many immigrants we (as a country) can allow to enter without adversely affecting the well-being of those are already here.

All alternate family/household forms are responses to personal images of marriage. Trying to distort and "adulterate" marriage by purporting a same-sex relationship as a "marriage" is another expression of our human sinful desire to redesign God's creation in our own image, rather than to seek to love God more "nearly, dearly, and clearly," as the classical prayer seeks.

We are clearly in favor of a new "equal regard" marriage with cooperation, mutual respect, equal rights and responsibilities for wife and husband, flexibility of roles, and emphasis on the quality of ways each spouse lives and works. In support of marriage and health we must not fall back into unjust marriage structures such as patriarchal marriage and divisions of roles based on gender. For marriage to become what God intended requires a "new man" and a "new woman" for a "new marriage" between a woman and a man who are co-equal as envisioned by God. The equalitarian concepts of "critical familism," "social partnership," and "progressive familism" apply to all dimensions of marriage, including legal contract, financial partnership, sacred promise, sexual union, personal bond, and a productive institution for society. [27] With these dimensions, our understanding of marriage must continue to develop and grow.[28]

References

Allen, Joseph L. *Love and Conflict: A Covenantal Model of Christian Ethics*. Lanham, Md.: University Press of America, 1955.

Bailey, D. S. *The Mystery of Love and Marriage. A Study in the Theology of Sexual Relation*. New York: Harper & Bros., 1952.

———. *Homosexuality and the Western Christian Tradition*. New York: Longmans, Green, 1955.

———. *Sexual Ethics: A Christian View*. New York: Macmillan, 1963.

Browning, Don. "What Is Marriage? An Exploration." Paper presented at the Institute for American Values Marriage Consultation, New York City, January 25, 2000.

Browning, Don S., Bonnie J. Miller-McLemore, Pamela D. Couture, K. Brynoll Lyon, and Robert M. Franklin. *From Culture Wars to Common Ground: Religion and the American Family Debate*. Louisville, Ky.: Westminster John Knox Press, 1997.

Browning, Don, and John Wall, eds. *Marriage, Health, and the Professions: The Implications of the Health Benefits of Marriage for the Practice of Law, Medicine, Ministry, Therapy, and Business*. Grand Rapids, Mich.: W. B. Eerdmans, 2001.

Bushnell, H. *Christian Nurture*. Cleveland, Ohio: The Pilgrim Press, 1994.

Coe, B. W. *John Wesley and Marriage*. Bethlehem: Lehigh University Press, 1996.

Coolidge, David O. "Justice for Marriage." *Family Policy* 14, no. 2 (March-April 2001): 2-6.

Diamant, Louis, and Richard D. McAnulty, eds. *The Psychology of Sexual Orientation, Behavior, and Identity.* Westport, Conn.: Greenwood Press, 1995.

Everett, W. J. *Blessed Be the Bond: Christian Perspectives on Marriage and the Family.* Philadelphia, Pa.: Fortress Press, 1985.

Fowler, J. W. *Faithful Change: The Personal and Public Challenges of Postmodern Life.* Nashville: Abingdon Press, 1996.

Friedman, Edwin. *Generation to Generation: Family Process in Church and Synagogue.* New York: Guilford Press, 1985.

Glendon, Mary Ann, and David Blankenhorn, eds. *Seedbeds of Virtue: Sources of Competence, Character, and Citizenship in American Society.* Lanham, Md.: Madison Books, 1995.

Gottman, J. M. *What Predicts Divorce? The Relationship Between Marital Processes and Marital Outcomes.* Hillside, N.J.: Lawrence Erlbaum, 1994.

———, *Why Marriages Succeed or Fail . . . And How You Can Make Yours Last.* New York: Simon & Schuster, 1994.

Haughton, J. B. "A Theology of Marriage." In *Male and Famale: Christian Approaches to Sexuality.* Ed. R. T. Barnhouse and U. T. Holmes, III. New York: Seabury Press, 1976.

Hunt, Joan A., and Richard A. Hunt. *Growing Love in Christian Marriage, Couples Book.* Rev. ed. Nashville: Abingdon Press, 2001.

Hunt, Richard A. "Marriage as Dramatizing Theology." *Journal of Pastoral Care* 41, no. 2 (June 1987): 119-31.

Hunt, Richard A., Larry Hof, and Rita DeMaria. *Marriage Enrichment: Preparation, Mentoring, and Outreach.* Philadelphia, Pa.: Brunner/Mazel, 1998.

Ives, Clifford, and Jane Ives. *Growing Love in Christian Marriage, Pastors and Leaders Book.* Rev. ed. Nashville: Abingdon Press, 2001.

Jewett, Paul K. *Man as Male and Female: A Study in Sexual Relationships from a Theological Point of View.* Grand Rapids, Mich.: W. B. Eerdmans, 1973.

Kasper, W. *Theology of Christian Marriage.* New York: Crossroads Publishing, 1981.

Kroeger, Charles C. "Are Gay Unions Christian Covenants?" In *Caught in the Crossfire.* Ed. Sally Geis. Nashville: Abingdon Press, 1994.

Lee, Cameron. *Beyond Family Values: A Call to Christian Virtue.* Downers Grove, Ill.: InterVarsity Press, 1998.

Lewis, Jerry M. *Marriage as a Search for Healing: Theory, Assessment, and Therapy.* New York: Brunner/Mazel, 1997.

Mack, Dana, and David Blankenhorn, eds. *The Book of Marriage: The*

Wisest Answers to the Toughest Questions. Grand Rapids, Mich.: W. B. Eerdmans, 2001.

"The Marriage Movement: A Statement of Principles." For full text, see www.marriagemovement.org

Nelson, J. B. *Embodiment: An Approach to Sexuality and Christian Theology.* Minneapolis: Augsburg Publishing House, 1978.

———. *Body Theology.* Louisville, Ky.: Westminster John Knox Press, 1992.

Olthus, J. H. *Keeping Our Troth: Staying in Love Through the Five Stages of Marriage.* San Francisco: Harper & Row, 1986.

Popenoe, David, Jean Bethke Elshtain, and David Blankenhorn, eds. *Promises to Keep: The Decline and Renewal of Marriage in America.* Lanham, Md.: Bowman & Littlefield, 1996.

Popenoe, David, and Barbara Dafoe Whitehead. *The State of Our Unions.* New Brunswick, N.J.: The National Marriage Project, 1999.

Socarides, Charles W. "Homosexuality Is Not Just an Alternative Lifestyle." In *Male and Famale: Christian Approaches to Sexuality.* Ed. R. T. Barnhouse and U. T. Holmes, III. New York: Seabury Press, 1976.

Sample, Tex, and Amy E. DeLong, eds. *The Loyal Opposition: Struggling with the Church on Homosexuality.* Nashville: Abingdon Press, 2000.

Schneider, Carl E. "The Law and the Stability of Marriage: The Family as a Social Institution." In *Promises to Keep: The Decline and Renewal of Marriage in America.* Ed. Popenoe, et al.

Stott, John. *Same-Sex Partnerships? A Christian Perspective.* Grand Rapids, Mich.: F. H. Revell, 1998.

Waite, Linda J., and Maggie Gallagher. *The Case for Marriage.* New York: Doubleday, 2000.

Wilcox, W. B. "For the Sake of the Children?" Manuscript draft prepared June 2000 for the Public Role of Mainline Protestantism project. Robert Wuthnow, principal investigator.

Witte, John, Jr. *From Sacrament to Contract: Marriage, Religion, and Law in the Western Tradition.* Louisville, Ky.: Westminster John Knox Press, 1997.

PART V: MINISTRY

CHAPTER 12

Homosexuality

A Pastoral Point of View[1]

Robert L. Kuyper

*T*he basic principles of transformation in the New Testament are also found in the Wesleyan and the Recovery movements. People affected by homosexuality are no different than others caught in addictions and problem behaviors. The same New Testament principles work to transform lives today just as they did in the past.

We read in Romans 12:2, "Do not be conformed to this world, but be transformed by the renewing of your minds." This is a command addressed to everyone! We all must move forward in transformation or risk conforming to the world. Paul is not speaking of homosexual people being transformed into heterosexuals since no one is singled out in this passage. All our lives are to be transformed. As we deal with the root desires and traumas of our lives, the desire to act out homosexually disappears. Just as the caterpillar turns into a butterfly, our lives are changed.

The same Greek word for transformation is used for Jesus in the Transfiguration. The change of glory in our Lord reminds us of our eventual final transformation. Paul speaks of reflecting the Lord's glory as we are being transformed (1 Cor. 3:18). The process of change is, more often than not, gradual, for we are *being* transformed. We are transformed by the "renewing of our minds" as old thought patterns are erased and new ones are learned.

John Wesley, who founded the Methodist movement, preached these same biblical principles for transforming the lives of converts in eighteenth-century England. In a time when people were being displaced by the Industrial Revolution and families were breaking down in the move to the cities, Wesley founded groups, the Methodist class system, that allowed persons to support one another in their attempts to improve their lives. People beset with temptations found support, and people could "bear one another's burdens" (Gal. 6:2). Honesty and accountability were key concepts that allowed the class system to work.

Alcoholics Anonymous uses this same honest sharing and accountability and the same biblical principles to transform the lives of alcoholics. At first shunned by professional therapists, this approach is now widely accepted by most. The same principles have been applied to substance and sexual addictions. Most ministries to homosexual people apply the same concepts. Now it is a badge of honor to be a recovering alcoholic; one day it will be the same for recovering homosexual people.

My personal experience confirms the power of these methods. As I learned more about the ex-gay movement, I found I had much in common with former homosexual men. I feared I was not masculine enough to meet our society's ideal male image. While they sought masculinity in sex with other men, I sought it in power over women. Desire for women other than my wife kept me from progressing in my walk with God. In a workshop led by Andy Comiskey of Desert Streams Ministry in Anaheim, I felt that desire being lifted out of me. My sexual brokenness was gone. I know that transformation happens; it happened to me!

If our churches are to minister to sexually broken people, we must recover these principles that John Wesley initiated and utilized. We live in a sexually dysfunctional society, in which molestation, rape, incest, and extramarital sex are the order of the day. We must minister in a world broken by the sexual revolution. The United Methodist Church cannot stand by and not offer help.

A Dysfunctional Church

It is unfortunate that the problems of the world have come into the church, just as they did in the New Testament. For example, we face an epidemic of clergy sexual misconduct. Heterosexual problems are much greater than homosexual ones. Yet we focus on the issue of homosexuality, perhaps to take our minds off much more serious sexual problems. A dysfunctional congregation will transform no one.

"Dysfunctional" has become a buzz phrase, but it simply means, *It does not work.* A broken-down automobile is dysfunctional because it cannot provide its basic function, transportation. American society is dysfunctional about sexuality. Instead of being a spiritual and physical binding force to create and maintain a marriage and family, sex becomes a commodity to sell merchandise. Women and children become victims as fathers are encouraged to abandon their families. We are admonished in the Bible to look out for widows and orphans. Today we create orphans and widows with our immorality. The economic consequences of this morality alone make this one of the most pressing issues in our society.

The sexual revolution of the sixties and seventies taught free love and sexuality without consequences. The children have paid the price. But we have reached a turning point as we do with all revolutions. The sexual revolution is coming to an end. Yet many do not know this. The conservative church is silent on morality, except to point out a few scapegoats. The liberal church is still in the 1960s. The church is dysfunctional in the midst of great need as we fail to carry out our basic purpose of transforming lives.

One of the marks of a dysfunctional family is the "don't talk" rule. Families in crisis never discuss their problems. Terrible things happen, but no one talks about it. Children learn not to trust their emotions and not to feel. Churches also observe this "don't talk" rule. We fail to address burning issues of the day concerning morality. Children and youth are left with no guidance. Families are left with no support.

Breaking Dysfunctional Patterns

For example, if in a United Methodist worship service, a woman stands and asks for prayer for her son who has just been diagnosed with cancer, she will receive support and compassion. But let her stand and ask for prayer for her son who she has just learned is gay, and her request will likely be met with silence. That is not an average request, and therein lies much of our problem with homosexuality. The woman whose son has cancer would receive much comfort and support, as we "bear one another's burdens" in our fellowship. What support will the family who has a member in the homosexual lifestyle receive?

We begin breaking dysfunctional patterns simply by talking about them. Thereby, we break the "don't talk" rule. Bob Davies, the former executive director of Exodus International, refers to "breaking the sound barrier," that is, referring to the matter from the pulpit or in the church newsletter.[2] Just by discussing the Christian response to homosexuality, we break the rule of secrecy in our dysfunctionality. When we begin to name and examine homosexuality, people feel free to come for help, because they now feel they can trust us enough to reveal their secrets. Like the mother above, they feel they can discuss family problems, and even their own struggles with us. The "don't talk, don't trust, don't feel," cycle has been broken. We are on our way to healing.

Telling stories of those who have overcome a struggle with homosexuality or any other form of sexual brokenness can be a powerful aid in breaking dysfunctionality. When the prophet Nathan confronted King David with his adultery, Nathan told the king a story about a man whose only sheep was stolen by a rich man. King David recognized himself in the story. Stories have a way of sneaking past our defenses; no wonder the comics can be so effective. In the guise of harmless humor, the comics often make telling points about life. The success of *Peanuts* cartoons in proclaiming the gospel to an unbelieving world would be one example.

Personal stories are also effective. Much of the time spent in Alcoholics Anonymous is with persons sharing their struggles and how they overcome their addiction. As persons share in those groups, "cross talk" is not allowed. Cross talk is advice on how to fix the problem. AA is not a therapy group. We do not try to fix others; that can become enabling. Instead, an atmosphere that allows our personal journeys to be shared is created. We all learn from one another.

We should stop scapegoating the gay and lesbian community. They are not to blame for all our family problems. The sexual revolution brought on sexual brokenness. Promiscuity, abortion, and homosexuality are the symptoms of a sexual brokenness. This means we will not attack gay and lesbian people as "the enemy." We will not tell offensive jokes that stereotype gay men and lesbians.

Such jokes and unfair comments will keep people from coming to us for help. We may not endorse every item of the gay agenda, but we will treat homosexual persons as "persons of sacred worth."

We also need to stop enabling behavior. Many gay and lesbian people are convinced that it is impossible for them to change. They go through many rationalizations, a kind of "stinkin' thinkin'," to convince themselves they cannot change. We probably will not "win" any arguments with them on this subject, but we can let them know that we believe change is both desirable and possible. When they hear of those who have changed, they may argue that those who changed were not "real" homosexuals. Since we cannot otherwise identify "real" homosexuals, how do we know who the "real" homosexual is. It becomes just a matter of semantics; the "real" homosexual is one who has not changed. But anyone might change in the future. We need to gently hold out the hope of change.

A Transforming Ministry

There is a United Methodist Church in practically every town and city in the United States. We have great resources in people, programs, and property. We should be making as much impact as John Wesley's classes did in England. We are a sleeping giant.

Many churches even in rural areas have found that they have parents with sons and daughters who are homosexual. Often, these children live elsewhere, perhaps in a big city. The parents suffer in silence with no support. There should be a support group for parents in every town. If your town does not have one, this is likely a needed ministry.

Parents and others affected by homosexuality need information. Churches and pastors can keep books and other information in church libraries and provide them for those who make their concerns known. Information can be shared with the congregation, making it possible for those who need it to seek help. Parents blame themselves. It is comforting to just say that it is not one's fault and that it is all due to inheritance. We cannot always explain why someone is homosexual. Parents do the best they can. If they made mistakes, they need to seek forgiveness, as we all do.

Parents and family members need to be encouraged to keep the relationship open with their homosexual family members. It rarely works to talk someone out of homosexuality. We need to wait for them to "hit bottom" then be ready to offer help when it is asked for. The transforming congregation challenges the myth that homosexual persons cannot change. This is part of the renewal of our minds. We seek to get information out to our communities and our denominations. The transforming congregation offers a warm and welcoming place to those affected by sexual brokenness. Yet at the same time, we should resist condoning sinful behavior. Like our Lord, we should say, "Neither do I condemn you. Go your way, and from now on do not sin again" (John 8:11).

A transforming congregation will also stand ready to be a friend to those who are struggling with homosexuality. A person leaving homosexuality behind has little chance of success without forming friends in a new lifestyle. Church members can be those friends. We need to realize that everyone will not be ready to share openly with the entire congregation at first. We can encourage sharing in small groups to gain support of a few supportive friends who can hold us all accountable. We are often eager to have a former homosexual share the story of their transformation. Many are not ready to share, for this often exposes a person to questioning and even discrimination. Often the struggler is ready, but family members are not. We need to respect boundaries and privacy.

One need not be an expert on homosexuality to be a friend. Many churches have sponsors for new members to help them learn their way around the church and its activities. In the same way, a friend can disciple the person leaving homosexuality behind. Encourage him or her to join Bible study groups and support groups that the church may offer. Friends provide a place for honesty and model appropriate gender behavior and same-sex friendships. Friends are part of an accountability system and a discipleship process. If there were more congregations involved in such transforming ministry with waiting and willing friends, even more people would be successful in leaving behind their struggles with homosexuality and sexual brokenness.

We face the choice created as the prodigal son returned home. We can either be the loving father who throws a party, or we can be the condemning elder brother who is unhappy at his brother's return. The Lord brought the prodigal to his senses. We cannot do that. But the prodigal sons and daughters are returning home. Will we welcome them in The United Methodist Church?

CHAPTER 13

Race and Sex in the Debate over Homosexuality in The United Methodist Church

Edward P. Wimberly

*U*nlike other ideologies that dehumanize and demonize people for their differences, The United Methodist Church's convictions about homosexuality are grounded in the concern for the growth and development of the image of God inherent in all of God's people. This brief essay contrasts The United Methodist Church's stated convictions about homosexuality, the ordination of homosexuals, and the marriage of persons of the same sex, with the oppressive and repressive racist, sexist, and patriarchal ideologies. The argument of this essay is that our denomination's convictions on these important issues are founded in a holistic theological anthropology as well as in the significant doctrines of justification and sanctification.[1]

Racism is the conviction that one race is superior to another based on biological skin color and implies the power to enforce such a conviction in everyday life. Similarly, sexism is the conviction that one gender is inherently superior to the other based on biology. Negative attitudes toward homosexuality (sometimes called "homophobia") are grounded in the belief that persons with same-sex preferences are inherently inferior to persons who are heterosexual. Political, social activist, and theological stances

153

opposing these ideologies are generally correct because such pejorative convictions are not only erroneous and unjust, but theologically incorrect as well.

It is the argument of this essay that The United Methodist Church's convictions about homosexuality are *not* grounded in an ideology of scarcity, in which God's love is available to some but not to others. Rather, our denomination's convictions are based on the theological belief that all persons are created in the image and likeness of God, and that our worth and dignity are unlimited gifts from God. Such gifts need not be hoarded or protected from extinction. It is through the life, death, and resurrection of Jesus Christ that these unlimited resources become universal gifts from God, extended to all humankind regardless of race, gender, or even sexual orientation.

The foundation for the conviction that dignity and worth are gifts of God is the Wesleyan theology of sanctification. In Wesleyan theology, the gift that bestows dignity and worth to all God's creations is justification, the beginning process of salvation. The process of salvation involves continued growth and development of persons toward the completeness and wholeness of God's image. This process is known as sanctification.[2] In Wesleyan theology, certain practices, sexual or otherwise, can block the process of human fulfillment and development. Consequently, The United Methodist Church's convictions about homosexuality assume a Wesleyan orientation toward salvation and presuppose a concern for continued growth and development of the image of God in all persons as they move toward completion and wholeness.

Homosexuals are, according to The United Methodist Church's published statements, "individuals of sacred worth."[3] Their sexual orientation or impulses do not change that. Also, they are persons who can grow in becoming more of what God intended them to be. Like all other persons, they are not victims of their passions; they are worthy of being created in God's image. While neither they nor their nonhomosexual counterparts will ever be "perfect" this side of death, they are able to develop toward the ideal.

Biases and Their Source

All convictions have certain sources, especially those beliefs that shape our views on sexuality. My convictions stem from the local and contextual theologies I heard growing up as I listened to my parents' stories and sayings. My father was very clear in his feelings about homosexuality, and he was always consistent when we asked him about certain people in our family. He would say that homosexuality was a private affair between God and the person and that the person had to deal with God about his or her own behavior. My father would emphasize that homosexuals are children of God and are recipients of God's grace. Never once did I hear him bash or condemn homosexuals. At the same time, I never heard him endorse the homosexual lifestyle. In general, I believe he and my mother knew that they had to be careful about what they said on the subject of homosexuality because of relatives and friends who were homosexual. They wanted us to be open. They did not want us to discriminate or be unjust. Our family had endured enough of this, and we did not want to engage in exclusionism.

I have not always had a traditional attitude toward homosexuality. I am a proud alumnus of Boston University School of Theology where openness toward gay and lesbian people and issues was expected. To be on the cutting edge of social and justice issues was expected as well. When I finished seminary, I became fully involved in social issues through my work as an urban minister. I was exposed to gay and lesbian issues through seminars, acquaintances, and friends who began to come out publicly about their homosexuality. As a Boston University School of Theology alumnus and as a member of the then Southern New England Conference of The United Methodist Church, I fully supported the concerns and aspirations of homosexuals.

In 1975, my attitude and stance began to change when I left New England and came South to The Interdenominational Theological Center (The ITC). I brought with me my liberal attitudes and disposition toward homosexuality. In fact, I supervised a student who was counseling gay couples and was pastoring at a Metropolitan Community Church. I began to change my point of view to more traditional convictions because of the many homosexual students who came to me for pastoral counseling, desiring not to be in the homosexual lifestyle. Although I have never attempted to "convert" gay or lesbian persons from the gay or lesbian lifestyle, many of my counselees convinced me that they had tried to come out and accept their homosexuality. However, they insisted that they could not escape the feeling that they could not be ethical Christians and continue in this lifestyle. I learned from most of them that homosexuality is extremely complicated, a life-long struggle that cannot be easily resolved by deciding to come out or by affirming one's heterosexuality. They taught me not to be blinded by popular beliefs and to enter their pain and struggles. As a result, I am convinced that a traditional, orthodox view of homo-sexuality, though experienced as oppressive to some, can be liber-ating for others who are struggling to conform their lives to what they think the gospel demands.

An Argument from Sanctification

One assumption I bring to interpreting Scripture is the belief that we are story-shaped human beings whose behavior is informed by convictions and beliefs related to the narratives of our faith tradi-tion. Part of what we are today in our ministries is informed by a complex history of ideas; yet there are historians who help us dis-cern some of the patterns of our story. One such pattern in the his-tory of practical theology in The United Methodist Church is an emphasis on sanctification. Historian E. Brooks Holifield summa-rizes the history of ideas informing this emphasis on sanctification. The emphasis grew out of a seventh-century preoccupation with "willful egocentricity" and "self-centeredness," and sanctification was viewed as a way of overcoming our self-centered self-interest.[4] Therefore, Holifield concludes that sanctification became a process of overcoming our lower, base motivations and putting in their place higher motivations: "Spiritual growth meant a process of 'sanctification,' empowered by supernatural grace, which created in the soul a capacity to obey and honor the highest-ranking of all hierarchical beings."[5]

With the dawning of the twentieth century came shifts in the notions of self-centeredness, and a new emphasis emerged, in which religion and morality were viewed as hindrances to self-realization due to the conformity of the self to social expectations that submerged individuality.[6] Therefore, Holifield concludes that we have moved from an emphasis on sanctification that sought to overcome self-centeredness, to self-realization as a means of freeing the self from authoritarian structures.[7]

Holifield's book was completed in 1983, and I want to argue that we have moved into the postmodern period since that time.

Sanctification has reappeared in the form of a rediscovery of the need for participation rather than self-growth and development apart from community. Postmodernity emphasizes the human need to be part of a significant community and to be shaped by its story. In this context, sanctification has shifted from an emphasis on overcoming self-centeredness to a narrative-shaped person empowered by the Holy Spirit toward completeness and wholeness. This puts the Church's teaching on homosexuality in a new light. Better said, it is a renewed emphasis on an old light—the light John Wesley discovered in his cell groups. The Church today needs to incorporate homosexuals, along with all other Christians seeking to grow in grace, into sharing groups for support, courage, and inspiration. Herein, homosexuals and other Christians can learn a new story and become participants in the fellowship of the Church.

In the postmodern narrative orientation, the emphasis is on the fact that our entire lives are shaped by the presence of God through the Holy Spirit transforming our natures and developing the image of God within each person. Thus, the goal is human growth and development of the image of God that is within each person.

The emphasis of sanctification on the growth and development of the God-image within through participation in community focuses on inclusion and not exclusion. Consequently, the concern is not on saving the scarce resources of dignity, as is the case with racism, sexism, homophobia, or heterosexism. Rather, postmodern sanctification assumes that the resources of dignity and worth are unlimited and that the development of the image of God within is the work of the church.

My studies of the historical Jesus convince me that all persons, regardless of race, gender, or sexual orientation, have access to God's gifts of identity, worth, and dignity. Only God can provide the gift of value inherent in our being created in God's own image and likeness. Not only is the access to God's gift of worth and value unlimited, the supply is unlimited as well.

I am convinced that The United Methodist Church's stand on sexuality reflects this postmodern understanding of sanctification. The emphasis is on inclusion and participation, recognizing that the development of the image of God in persons is a gradual process that necessitates a loving and caring community. Our legislated convictions on homosexuality are rooted in the highest motives related to the doctrine of sanctification, which emphasizes the need for persons to become more Christlike, fully developing in the image of God.

There are several features to the sanctification position I am advocating. First, it removes the pressure of needing to "change" the homosexual. Sanctification is a process through which God transforms us through the power of the Word as narrative. Second, it moves beyond what Larry Graham calls rejection toward a "rejection non-punitive and qualified acceptance" point of view. This approach "accepts the heterosexual norm for sexual behavior though recognizing that homosexuals are children of God belonging to God's family."[8]

Conclusion

There will be many homosexuals who feel excluded from The United Methodist Church because of its convictions about homosexuality. Because of this reality, our denomination needs to be in continuous dialogue. I firmly believe that most of our problems in the area of human sexuality, whether homosexual or heterosexual, are related to the fact that the village has broken up worldwide, and sex has become a means, albeit inadequate, of restoring community. Most of us are *relational refugees,* cut off from genuine community and seeking a genuine relationship wherever we can find it. The Church should address our relational isolation not through propositions, but through offering genuine relationships firmly grounded in a narrative approach that mediates God's unlimited gift of human worth and dignity developed through participation in a caring and sanctifying community.

CHAPTER 14

The Incompatibility of Homosexuality and the Church

Thoughts from the Church in the Developing World

Gershon and Gladys Mwiti

Introduction

But in the prophets of Jerusalem
I have seen a more shocking thing:
they commit adultery and walk in lies;
they strengthen the hands of evildoers,
so that no one turns from wickedness;
all of them have become like Sodom to me,
and its inhabitants like Gomorrah.
(Jer. 23:14)

*H*omosexuality is not the only depravity the church has to look into in this context. Each immorality has other related evils that go with it. Homosexuality in churches therefore is a reflection of deeper problems in a church that has been undermining spiritual nourishment of her sheep. It reflects a culture of rationalism, pluralism, enlightenment, and excessive freedom all aping modern civilization. Homosexuality cannot therefore be discussed in isolation. To do so would be tantamount to dealing with an undiagnosed disease by treating symptoms instead of the cause. As Paul wrote to Timothy:

> You must understand this, that in the last days distressing times will come. For people will be lovers of themselves, lovers of money, boasters, arrogant, abusive, disobedient to their parents, ungrateful, unholy, inhuman, implacable, slanderers, profligates, brutes, haters of good, treacherous, reckless, swollen with conceit, lovers of pleasure rather than lovers of God, holding to the outward form of godliness but denying its power. Avoid them! (2 Tim. 3:1-5)

The church in the West need not be reminded that all forms of modern education, science, and technology have their origin in the church. However, stealthily and systematically, through the years, the church has lost her hold not just on educational institutions but also on the content of education curricula. The loss goes beyond institutions of secular learning to theological seminaries, which, although founded by the church and once belonged to her, no longer are hers. Education is a voice that shapes society, and this utterance was church based, loud and clear. At one point in history, the church spoke, and the world listened. Today—alas!—it is the reverse. The world speaks and the church pays attention. It seems that all the church can do now is oppose motions tabled by others. For example, in matters of world politics, economics, ecology, sociology, philosophy, and even creation and theology, all the church can do now is mainly react to what the world proposes. This situation includes homosexuality, our subject here.

Homosexuality is not a proposal from within the church, but an external world dictate that is fast becoming a main agenda of the church in the West. It is a motion powerful enough to rip its way through whatever the church has held dear, including fellowship, gentleness, love, and common grace. However, to date, what the church is doing is simply reacting and not understanding the root cause of the problem. As the world flies off in her spiritual search for technological creations, a deflated church crawls spiritually and sits back to hear the next prescription the world is likely to hand to her so that she can adjust herself accordingly. She finds herself emotionally weakened, a state that justifies and makes room for homosexuality from the pew to pulpit. To single out and table homosexuality as an agenda in the church is a clear declaration of defeat before the battle.

What are the imminent implications? We might assume that with the current trend, it is only a matter of time before the church again opens her doors to adultery, prostitution, fornication, and other practices that no longer raise eyelids. The next agenda after this may well be murder, theft, or bearing false witness—practices that will be accepted as a normative for Christian practice, just as abortion no longer raises concerns. Eventually, all sins will be justified and the church will grind into apostasy. This is the trend that will rationalize the Scriptures, molding the Word to fit into our culture instead of transforming culture to be subservient to the Word.

Homosexuality Viewed from Cultural and Church Standpoints

In general, most developing countries do not have an equivalent word for homosexuality. The practice can only be described in many words, suggesting that it does not exist. Many people we questioned confessed that they got the notion of homosexuality through reading Western books or hearing stories about it. Where and if it is cited in the culture, it is always associated with *cursed* people. Many cultures consider it taboo for any person to deviate from the normal and natural human behavior. Among the Meru of Kenya, for example, such a person would be called *uturutu,* a name also given to a goat that behaves unlike other goats, sometimes sitting down like a dog, and so on. An animal that gets itself into this behavior is labeled a *uturutu* and killed to protect other animals against imitating uturutu. Homosexuality is therefore understood to be a deviation from what is normal and, therefore, is *uturutu,* an abomination, whether practiced by a Christian or a nonbeliever. How one acquires the behavior—innate or learned—is immaterial. What matters is that it is a deviation, and many in the developing world would argue that if God meant it to be so, he would have made it obvious at creation!

161

It follows then that, culturally, the developing world has certain things that are unutterable in the presence of respectable people. Homosexuality is one of them. Such a mention would be termed *kugumuka* among the Meru people and in many other African communities. For example, to say what should not be spoken, or allow the conception of a thought that should be stopped, is tantamount to walking naked in the public. Stopping thoughts before they become actions is an indication of self-control, an ingrained behavior that is acquired through training and retraining, especially through rites of passage. Many African cultures seem to adhere to a Judeo-Christian value system. They underline cultural expectations with biblical admonitions, such as "do not even eat with such a one" (1 Cor. 5:11*b*) and that self-control is a fruit of the spirit (Gal. 5:22).

Most of the developing countries have very strong nuclear and extended family ties, through which this training and retraining takes place. Within the family, a deviant would be considered a black sheep to be disowned and possibly stoned to death for dishonoring the family. Family honor is paramount and supersedes personal pleasure and desirability. It is out of this context that the African *Umuntu,* a philosophy *of* "I am, because we are," arises.[1] It is a fundamental and culturally loaded statement implying that no one can live and exist alone. We all need one another, and therefore the suffering of one is the suffering of all. The deviance of one is the deviance of all. This presupposes the need to protect and to be responsible for one another in the community. This connectedness underlines the place of culture at family, clan, and community levels. It also emphasizes a training that people should live responsibly, thinking of the whole unit and not just individual concerns. This concern for community wellness may look like self-denial, but it forms the fundamental difference between the West and developing worlds in terms of culture and elements that make society. This is emphasized by John Stott when he reportedly stated in a speech, "In the East, all there is unity without freedom, while in the West, it is all freedom, without unity." However, in between is the church, a living organ that has both unity and freedom. The freedom of the Bible is guaranteed—"The truth will make you free" (John 8:32*b*). Therefore, although there are two basic norms that seem to differentiate cultural and behavioral expectations in the West versus other cultures, the middle position of the church maintains both, a position that the way of the Christian faith should offer redemption and responsible freedom to all.

To find what international Christian leaders are saying about homosexuality, we conducted a brainstorming session with a few persons from Africa, Asia, the Middle East, and Latin America—all visitors in the United States. Out of their contribution, two views emerged: a stand within the Pentecostal churches, and the perception of mainline churches such as Methodist, Anglican, Presbyterian, Baptist, Lutheran, Mennonite, and so on. In both views, the link between the church and culture was strong, in that Christianity was brought into cultures that already had their own values and virtues, rules and regulations and laws, character and behavior. These are the foundational pillars on which faith in Christ within the developing nations stands and should be grounded.

The perceptions of the Pentecostal churches were rooted both in cultural values and in the teaching of the Bible, which were central in whatever this group presented. The basic questions they raised were "What does the Bible say about homosexuality?" and "Is what the Bible says consistent with our cultural value system?" For example, the following Scriptures were cited as biblical behavior that is bulwarked by cultural expectations:

1 Corinthians 6:18-20—Flee from sexual immorality.
James 1:14-16—But each one of us is tempted.
1 Corinthians 7:2-5—Each man should marry a woman.

Therefore, to the Pentecostals, homosexuality is not an issue worthy of discussion by the church because it is unthinkable and the church has more pressing and relevant issues to ponder. To these leaders, prevention is better than cure. Where Bible studies, prayer meetings, fellowships, and preaching of the Word are intensified with clean motives within a community with a value system of accountability, this alone saves the church from the rigors of homosexuality, pornography, and other related appetites of the body.

Closely related to homosexuality is the issue of immorality in any form. The stand of the church is clear. The emphasis overall is holiness, purity of heart, and righteousness as demanded by the Scriptures. The biblical stand on homosexuality is solid and cannot be compromised by the church. Upholding such a stringent value system does not mean that church members are perfect. Instead, it is an expectation that places upon the leadership the responsibility for training within church and community with the aim of becoming more like Christ and not giving in to the demands of the body that would lead to disobedience to God's law and the destruction of family and society.

The leaders of the mainline churches expressed the fact that sin is sin in any way one chooses to look at it. The tendency to dilute the power of the Scriptures in order to accommodate certain personal wishes and preferences does not rule out the Scriptures' divine authority and unshakable stand. In the mainline churches, Christian disciplines are still strong and effective regardless of whether they are obeyed. These churches are more organized than the newer denominations and have structures that have a long history of guiding the practice of Christian faith and implementing doctrines that enhance this adherence.

Consequently, these structures are strong and respectable and have formulated guidelines with power and authority to rebuke, challenge, correct, discipline, and even excommunicate any deviants who persistently and notoriously choose to live lives that resist change and transformation. These churches operate as families operate, demanding demonstration of spiritual maturity in social justice, moral uprightness, and integrity of individual believers. Immorality is regarded as spiritual immaturity, which needs discipleship and deep teaching of the Scriptures. Homosexuality has not become an issue for church discussion.

When immorality is witnessed, the church retreats to check where it is failing in teaching, rebuking, correcting, and training (2 Tim. 3:16-17). Although the Christian faith welcomes all, people cannot continue to live within the church family and still practice adultery, fornication, prostitution, witchcraft; divorce and remarry multiple times; choose to have children out of wedlock; or engage in homosexuality. Continued presence of these sins with no transformation signals the church's inability to cause spiritual growth in its members and, therefore, the need to re-examine the mission and vision of the church as salt and light. Such members need tough love, care, and guidance because Christ sets us free from sin, and, in turn, the indwelling Holy Spirit produces in us the gift of self-control as we persistently live out our faith (Gal. 5:22). With this freedom, we can worship God in spirit and truth (John

4:23), neither deceiving ourselves nor being deceived (2 Tim. 3:13). Such a life denotes holiness, purity of heart, and righteousness in character. Homosexual persons still living lives in which they are not just entertaining but also expressing behaviors outside the boundaries that God has placed for us cannot be classified as Christian.

Therefore, whether within the mainline churches or among Pentecostal churches, the gospel preached in the developing world expects results that lead to salvation, repentance, forgiveness of sin, and freedom from all forms of bondage, including homosexuality. People cannot meet the Lord and remain the same. The Lord comes to loose chains and cause painful death to things of the past so that, dying to self with all its lusts and desires, one can be born again in the newness of life that depicts the new birth. Thieves do not steal any more. Those with stolen goods return those goods. Women living as concubines leave. The sexually immoral repent and change their lives. In essence, salvation is followed by an obvious transformation and public acknowledgment of what the Lord has done. Then follows discipleship within a caring group of believers, among whom the new convert is guided to put off the old self, "corrupt and deluded by its lusts," so that he or she can begin to be "renewed in the spirit of [his or her] minds" (Eph. 4:22-23). This newness of life involves a deliberate obedience, practicing Paul's continued admonition to "clothe yourselves with the new self, created according to the likeness of God in true righteousness and holiness" (Eph. 4:24).

Thoughts on Accountability—Stewardship of the Body

One's body belongs not only to oneself, but also to one's family, church, and community. This fact is affirmed by three human functions that are highly cerebrated and united as one: birth, baptism, and death. Whenever and wherever birth, baptism, or death occur, there is always a community concern expressed in joy or sorrow. This underscores peoples' connection with one another, an indication of belonging to one another in some crucial ways. When one person is sick, suffering, or going through trials and temptations, all those who know the individual are connected to him or her in that experience. In the same way, homosexuals create a concern to all who know them, particularly concerns about the way they abuse their bodies, which can lead to broken homes, confused children, and even the disease AIDS.

The concerns expressed in this chapter are a cry not to deny people pleasure, but to appeal to the church to open the eyes of the blind that "there is a way that seems right to a person, but its end is the way to death" (Prov. 14:12). When Paul talked of the need to "flee from sexual immorality" (1 Cor. 6:18), he was well aware that sexual sin not only affects the body but also transforms the whole system—body, mind, and spirit.

Many will argue that homosexuality should not be singled out of many other sins as if it were different; but in a way, homosexuality is different. Failure to realize the seriousness of its practice and acceptance represents a step lower into the downward spiral of depravity, which can water down the seriousness of its implications especially when the church begins to debate its inclusion in expectations of holy living. Why should homosexuality receive special treatment in this day and age?

1. The practice contradicts the natural order of sexuality within humanity and the rest of God's creation.
2. It is synonymous with sodomy. Sodomy is one of the dirtiest and most debasing actions any human being can dare.
3. Humanly speaking, homosexuality embarrasses victims and others wherever they are; it often places those who practice it perpetually on the defensive, trying to justify their behavior.
4. Biblically, homosexuality is classified along with adultery, whoremongery, sodomy, fornication, prostitution, witchcraft, and self-abuse.
5. It is a passion that gradually leads to self-destruction as it deceptively allures one to sickness and eventually death that can reach beyond the grave (Rev. 22:15).
6. Homosexuality as a practice has no virtue, except self-indulgence, and therefore needs no promotion in any capacity. Instead, it is an evil in society to be shunned and fought against with powers available in the church and elsewhere.
7. Homosexuals need love, care, and counseling. If after teaching and counseling they continue the practice, the

church should take a firm stand to rebuke, discipline, and excommunicate to save the church from contamination. The greatest kindness that we can sometimes do with people is "time out."

The Relationship Between the Northern and Southern Church

The church in the developing world views the church in the West as a parent deserving respect and appreciation for what she has been and still is. The church in the Third World owes a lot to the church in the West in terms of missionary work that demanded sacrifice, commitment, and love. It is only in a gentle spirit that the church in the developing world dare critique and rebuke the church in the West, because we all well know what it cost these brethren to bring the gospel to us. Yet, at times, there comes the need for a child to admonish a parent. We are aware that amidst much suffering, the West brought the gospel to us—the developing church—established churches, Bible schools, public schools, and hospitals—institutions that they continue to maintain long after the southern churches went autonomous. Western missionaries sacrificed families, property, and even their own lives in the process of establishing churches. For all this commitment, churches in the developing countries owe churches in the West many praises and thanks to God.

However, the introduction of homosexuality into a church's agenda, demanding attention in the church in the West, is viewed as humiliation to the church not just in developed nations, but in the world at large. According to the church in the developing world, homosexuality is part of a strategic plan by the enemy for the church worldwide. This emphasis is not a micro- but a macro-plan to dilute the power of the church on earth. It can be called, the devil's "religious ploy," an agenda presented cunningly to the church through various slogans that are becoming accepted today. For example, some believe that individual freedom should be *guaranteed* and that people have a right to personal happiness whatever that does to individuals or to the society at large.

This notion of guaranteed individual freedom is misleading and confusing when viewed from the spiritual standpoint. What makes it spiritually disgusting is the fact that such notions are held as truths, even in the household of faith, without realizing the erosion of values that the church has always held dear. Lowering standards for the sake of equality and freedom does not guarantee society will benefit overall. The right action is to lift standards where they are low without lowering the high ones.

Enabling the church to grow in developing countries is not growth at all. Both regions can and should grow simultaneously. This is more honorable. These slogans therefore should be fought and resisted by every Christian the world over. So, we beg to differ that the church in the West is not weak. This is a lie of the enemy. The church in the West is still the strongest. Why the conviction? It is a fact that the church in the West owns all church spiritual treasures of the world today. Among them is the historical heritage, church archives, and some of the oldest and greatest seminaries and institutions of higher learning. These treasures include literature that stretches to the fathers and mothers of the church, human treasures in forms of teachers and lecturers, and Christian scholarship. Economically, the church in the West is stronger now than in any other time in history. The enemy has blinded the church in the West.

We are convinced that the presence of homosexuality in the church is a divine voice that the church needs to heed. It could be an attempt for God to reveal the state of the church in the world—a body that has become spiritually porous, allowing the dictates of any theology cooked up by the mind. How secure is the church from the dictates of the culture in which she finds herself?

Conclusion

> *The nations raged,*
> *but your wrath has come,*
> *and the time for judging the dead,*
> *for rewarding your servants, the prophets*
> *and saints and all who fear your name,*
> *both small and great, and for destroying those who*
> *destroy the earth."*   *(Rev. 11:18)*

Traditionally, the church in the West has for centuries been viewed as a leader in all matters related to the church worldwide.

Whatever comes from Europe or North America has always been assumed to be good, needing no questioning. This leading role is now waning, placing the Western church in a questionable, precarious position. Homosexuality continues to embarrass the church in developing nations, an unmentionable, unimaginable feeling akin to seeing one's parent walking around naked, which is believed to make the child go blind. How dare our parents tell us that it is all right for brother to take brother to bed and sister to take sister to bed? What is this evil among us? The practice, therefore, stands out as one of the proposals awaiting heavy opposition from the rest of the world church, and it should not come to this. With the Wesleys and other great fathers and mothers of the faith, The United Methodist Church has been likened to a sleeping giant, and God now speaks to her. Is she listening?

PART VI: CHANGE

CHAPTER 15

Lesbian No More

Susan McDonald

My heart was in my throat as I stood at the microphone near the front of the huge chapel at the University of Redlands, which was filled to capacity with over a thousand delegates to our California-Pacific Annual Conference. Only moments before, the entire body had been presented with a series of quick skits, intended to illustrate the various ways the Church could minister to the needs of the communities around us. An old woman stood and told of feeling alone and afraid at the elder-care facility she lived in. A "church member" stood and told about the visitation ministry available at their church. He put his arm around her and left the stage. Another person stood as a child and spoke about how scary it was to be home alone after school, since her dad was gone and her mother had to be at work all day. This time a "church person" rose and spoke about the special program available for latchkey kids and took the hand of the "child" and led her away. After several of these vignettes, a young woman rose to speak. "I love the Lord and have a call in my life to ordination," she said. "I have my degree and have been going through the process for years. But the *Discipline* says I can't be ordained. I can't change the way I am. What am I supposed to do?" This time another "church person" stood and, without saying a word, put his arm around her as they walked away from the microphone. I sat there stunned and indignant, waiting to hear the outcry that would surely come from several people in the assembled body. This last skit was clearly intended to convey that homosexuality was something a person is born with, and that our church—The United Methodist Church, whose General Conference had confirmed our current *Discipline*, stating that homosexuals are persons of worth, and also that homosexuals cannot be ordained—should rethink its position on homosexuals and work to change or ignore our *Discipline* in favor of ordaining practicing gays and lesbians. I held my breath. I waited. Then the moment passed, and no voice was raised.

So only a minute later I was standing less than twenty feet from our bishop, who was presiding over the conference. On his collar, he was wearing the bright rainbow-hued ribbon that had suddenly become the symbol of gay support, much to the chagrin of many Christian souls who had participated in the Cursillo and Walk to Emmaus programs, at which the rainbow and the greeting "De Colores!" had become associated with a moving spiritual experience in their lives. Then I was given the floor. "Bishop, while your views about homosexuality are widely known, I represent many people here who still believe in and support our *Discipline*. I think it is inappropriate that you should sit in front of us all and preside over this annual conference wearing that ribbon." When I paused for a breath, I was amazed to see that the bishop's hands had flown to his collar, and the offending ribbon was off before I had finished speaking. But as bold as my words had been, they were only a gentle reproof compared to what I knew I had to say next. "Bishop, I stand before you as someone who lived as a lesbian for nearly ten years. I have left that lifestyle behind me and have been free of it for over twenty years now. How dare you permit people to propagate the lie that 'I can't change.'"

As I made my way back to my seat, the stunned silence that had followed my remarks turned to applause, which was quickly stifled by the bishop, who suggested a moment of silence. When I sat down, the hands of strangers reached out to touch me reassuringly, and gentle voices murmured things such as, "That was great!" and "You are so courageous!" I confess that I felt neither great nor courageous in that moment.

I am a fifty-something, white, middle-class person with an over-thirty daughter and a loving husband. I am a full-time technical writer for a large company, a part-time college student, and a some-time harpist. I serve in my church as a certified lay speaker, liturgist coordinator, and am the Lay Representative from our church at the Annual Conference. Before attending my first Annual Conference the year before, I considered myself a fairly "mainstream" Methodist, neither extremely liberal nor overly conservative concerning my own walk with the Lord. However, that first conference was a traumatic and heartbreaking experience for me and had led me directly to that microphone—to expose a secret that I had hardly thought about since I had abandoned the gay lifestyle so long ago.

Several events brought me to my feet to expose the lie that homosexuals are "born that way," or that there is a "gay gene." While this assertion is false and has been proved by several studies to be groundless, the supporters of the "gay agenda" have repeated it over and over until it is taken for truth. (These same supporters will swear there is no "gay agenda" either, which is another lie.) The first event, which I mentioned before, was the prior Annual Conference, where a whole series of gay agenda items had come before the conference. Those of us who raised any objections to this agenda were silenced, ignored, and generally prevented from injecting any perspectives. I was in tears before the first day of the conference was over. I felt betrayed by my own denomination and angry that Bible-believing people would tolerate what was happening.

During the year in between that first conference and the second one, I became part of a group of evangelical clergy and laypersons whose ideology lined up with my own. I listened to them struggle with how to combat the relentless movement away from biblical principles in the Methodist church, and agonize over ways to convince our gay brothers and sisters that we do love and want them to come to God, though maintaining that the Bible prohibits homosexuality.

In the middle of all the controversy, I came to the realization that no one was saying what I knew to be true—that many, many people can and do choose to leave the gay lifestyle. Homosexuals are telling everyone that they have no choice about their sexual preferences—and they must be the experts, right? The truth is that those of us who have left the lifestyle (and all the stigma it carries) behind are unwilling to stand and confess it. And so our silence leaves only the activists' voices incessantly drilling the same untruths into the public ear. My own past could provide the "secret weapon" that my God-loving, Bible-believing friends could use. I could stand and tell the truth that would silence that small voice that whispered in their ears, "What if they really *are* born gay?"

I have studied the Bible for many years now, and there are still many issues I struggle with. However God's plan for our sexuality isn't one of them. In passage after passage, the prohibitions against homosexuality are spelled out—for both men and women. The consequences for ignoring these prohibitions are also clearly illustrated. The gay agenda in our Church tries to re-interpret these damning Bible passages into something innocuous and pale, and they fall short of their goal. They have much more success at turning the minds and hearts of those in leadership in our Church toward amending our *Book of Discipline* to get rid of the—to them—offensive prohibitions against homosexuals being ordained or performing same-sex "marriages." They hate the statement that "the practice of homosexuality is incompatible with Christian teaching" because they want to be free to do what they want to do. The other thing they are very successful at is converting our youth, not to homosexuality necessarily, but to the belief that it's "OK to be gay."

When I was gay—for nearly all of my twenties—I repeated the story many times about how difficult the lifestyle was. I complained: "Do you think if I had a choice I would be this way?" and at the time, I believed it. Other gay men and women echoed the same sentiment all around me. We told it to one another and to anyone else who would listen. The lifestyle cost me many things. It alienated my family. I left my marriage. I gave custody of my eighteen-month-old daughter to my husband to avoid a court fight that I was certain to lose. I worked in an industry in which I was surrounded by "good old boys," and I lived in daily anxiety that one of them would discover my secret and corner me in some remote area of the plant. Many times I considered suicide. It was, looking back, the most horrible period of my life.

I would love to say that one day the Lord came into my life and changed it in an instant, but I think major lifestyle changes happen that way very rarely. It took a long time for me to realize that it wasn't true that I had to be gay. I finally came to the point that I was willing to be celibate the rest of my life, but I was not going to continue the way I had been. I had been far from the Lord for a long time, and still I turned to him in my darkest moments. I believe he worked in my life to bring me back to a path that led toward him. Over time, my relationship with my family was restored. I met and married a church-going man. Slowly, God restored the wasted years.

So many times we struggle through the hard times in our lives then are happy to put them behind us and never look back. However, it is just those difficult times that prepare us, all unknowing, to minister to others later. And so I believe this is the reason I have been invited to add my story to this book. I can say to persons who are currently trapped in the gay lifestyle, "It isn't true that you can't change! You are one of God's special, beloved children, and *you have a choice*! My own life is the truth of what I tell you." To my brothers and sisters in Christ I can say, "Stand firm! The Bible is true, and God's promises are true."

If we were discussing someone addicted to alcohol, or a friend who was having an affair, wouldn't it be the right thing to come alongside that person, put an arm around him or her and say, "You are going the wrong way, my friend"? It would be unthinkable to tell him or her that what he or she was doing was OK. Even if that person hated us for telling the truth, we would feel justified in dispensing "tough love," because of all the harm that will happen in that person's life if he or she is permitted to continue.

Telling a homosexual person that his or her lifestyle is OK or going along with the "gay agenda" is equally unthinkable. In doing so, you take away that person's option to come to the truth and return to a right relationship with fellow man and with the Creator. If we truly love him or her, as we profess to do, then we must continue to tell the truth and shine a light on the fact that they *do* have options. We cannot be persuaded to bend the principles laid down for us in the Bible in the name of "tolerance" or whatever other label the homosexual advocates would have us substitute for a lack of discernment. I do not hate gay persons; I personally know and love many of them. When I get to heaven, I want to see them there, wrap my arms around them, and say, "Welcome home!"

CHAPTER 16

Understanding and Treating the Lesbian Client[1]

Andria L. Signer-Small

Prologue

*I*magine entering the office of a pastor or Christian therapist, explaining your reasons for seeking help, and hearing responses similar to the following: "Most medical professionals believe that a change from a homosexual to a heterosexual orientation is really not possible. Biblically, many people believe that it is not even necessary. Have you considered the option of reconciling your homosexual orientation with your theology? Could it be possible that God created you this way and what would be your options if this were the case?" While a therapist might not state these ideas quite as blatantly, such opinions, nonetheless, are often communicated to lesbians distressed by their orientation.

If you believe, according to the Word of God, there is no need for individuals to seek change, this article may raise the following questions for you: *Why should people spend such time and energy endeavoring to change, especially with no guarantees of success? Why would they not, instead, choose to receive therapy to decrease guilt feelings, increase self-acceptance, and reconcile their theological perspectives with their lifestyle?*

However, for many who choose to attempt the process of change, the answers to these questions lie in their theology. They believe God's created intent for men and women is heterosexual and view homosexual desire or behavior as a part of their fallen nature, just like other aspects of our imperfect human nature. They are choosing to trust God's grace and actively embrace their process of sanctification.

My prayer is that as you read this "clinical" text, you would first understand the heart of the lesbian client who desires to align her lifestyle to her theology.

Why the Term "Lesbian"?

Recently, I was asked to critique an assessment tool used to measure change among individuals who had utilized psychotherapy to move from homosexuality to heterosexuality. In the first draft of the assessment's interview form, the questions appeared primarily oriented toward male homosexuals. Women responding to the questions as formulated would have measured a higher degree of change than actually achieved. The questions truly reflected an assumption that male and female homosexuality are essentially the same and simply involve same-gender, physical, and sexual attraction.

Although there may be etiological similarities in male and female homosexuality, there are gender-specific differences in the nature of these problems and in their outward manifestations. The gay community itself recognizes these differences. For this reason, many women prefer to be referred to as "lesbian" instead of "gay" or homosexual, and the popular public service organization is called The Gay and Lesbian Center.

Characteristics of Lesbian Relationships

Recognizing that there are exceptions to the common psychodynamics, I will briefly describe some of the distinct characteristics of female homosexual relationships.

The first characteristic—reflecting a basic difference between men and women—is that sex and sexual attraction are not necessarily key components of lesbian relationships. In many instances, the role of sex is minor and, occasionally, nonexistent. Instead, the physical activity more highly valued is holding and affection. In the cases that sex is a critical component, it is because of the emotional intimacy that it symbolizes. The propelling drive in the lesbian relationship is the woman's same-sex emotional and nurturing deficits, and these deficits are generally not sexualized to the same degree as they are in male homosexuality. For the female homosexual, "emotional attraction" plays a more critical role than does sexual attraction.

Next, within these relationships there appears to be a capacity for particularly strong attachment. However, a closer look reveals behaviors that indicate a fragile relational bond ridden with fear and anxiety. Core conflicts are evidenced in recurrent themes related to identity formation. For example, we see fears of abandonment or engulfment, struggles involving power (or powerlessness) and control, and desires to merge with another person to obtain a sense of security and significance.

Female relationships lean toward social exclusivity rather than inclusivity, and it is not unusual for a lesbian couple increasingly to reduce contact with family members and previous friends. This gradual withdrawal serves to ensure control and protects against separateness and perceived threats to their fragile bond.

While lesbian partnerships generally are of longer duration than male relationships, they tend to be fraught with emotional intensity and held together by the "glue" of jealousy, possessiveness, and various manipulative behaviors. During the course of the relationship, the "highs" are very high, and the times of conflict are extreme. Excessive time together, frequent telephoning, disproportionate card- or gift-giving, hastily moving in together or merging finances, are some of the ways separateness is defended against. In such relationships, we see the counterfeit of healthy attachment— that is, emotional dependency and overenmeshment.

It is not uncommon for lesbian lovers to have a "can't live if living is without you" feeling toward each other. A client once said to me, "I don't know how I would live without her. Before she came into my life, I was so empty. Now she is my life."

There is often a desperate quality to the emotional attraction in women that struggle with lesbianism. One client, who recognized that her lesbian relationships re-enacted her need for maternal love, explained to me, "When I meet a woman that I feel drawn to, it is as if a place inside me is saying, 'Will you be my mommy?' It is a compelling and powerful feeling, and a helpless one. Suddenly, I feel little. I want to be noticed by her, I want to be special to her, and that want takes over my mind."

Another client shared with me what it felt like during times of separation from her lesbian girlfriend. She said, "I remember feeling this terrible feeling—this gnawing, anxious feeling deep in the pit of my stomach. This is the same feeling I had as a child whenever I had to be away from home, or on the rare occasion I would attend a sleepover. The other girls would be having a blast, but all I wanted was to be home. It was always so hard to leave my mother."

Gender Identity and Lesbianism

What is easily observed among the lesbian population is a broad divergence of gender traits and outward appearances. Just as there are (paradoxically) heterosexually oriented women who are not "at ease" in their femininity, so too are there homosexually oriented women who enjoy being a woman and are highly feminine in appearance. I say this to dispel common thinking that a "boyish" appearance or the enjoyment of traditionally nonfeminine activities equals lesbianism.

Gender identity has to do with a woman's comfort with herself as a female, her level of ease in relating and identifying with other women, and the extent of her freedom-of-choice regarding female-oriented activities. Lesbianism is about a woman's same-gender preference for fulfillment of unconscious psychological longings and her fear of intimate connection with the opposite sex.

In lesbianism, a woman is developmentally "stuck" and therefore unable to move forward into healthy heterosexuality. However, when and how healthy development is thwarted would influence the degree of gender-identity problems experienced.

Anti-male Attitudes

Some lesbian women experience negative feelings and inner conflicts when relating to men, and this contributes to their inability to embrace heterosexuality. In addition, some strongly identify with radical feminism.

Women may be seen as gifted and desirable, though men are viewed as inferior, sex crazed, and somewhat useless. Describing a scene of a man and woman with their arms around each other at a baseball game, one lesbian client said, "It was so disgusting. All I could think was, *What does she see in him, and how could she let him touch her!*" It is not uncommon for those who have been involved in the lesbian lifestyle for a long period of time to increasingly experience an aversion to heterosexual relating.

Treatment Considerations

In order to treat the lesbian client who desires to embrace the change process, it is important to view her individually and to assess her as a whole person. Most important, the therapist must assess her personality organization. For example, does she have the separation-individuation conflicts of a borderline, the fragile self-esteem of a narcissist, or the attachment fears of a schizoid? Understanding the core conflicts will provide the therapist with the meaning behind the lesbian client's behaviors. With this information, it is possible to proceed utilizing appropriate interventions for this particular client.

Also important to notice is the degree of the client's compulsive or obsessive feelings, thoughts, and behaviors. The higher the compulsivity, the more anxiety and depression may surface as the client begins to separate from her lesbian partner or chooses not to "act out" her same-sex emotional attractions. This is often the most difficult part of treatment and strongly resembles the treatment required when struggling with substance addiction.

The gender of the therapist is critical; however, the lesbian client typically handles that concern herself, as her emotional attraction guides her to a woman therapist in the selection process. Over time, the client will attempt to act out, with the therapist, the same themes she enacted with her lesbian partners. For this reason, the therapist should demonstrate a relational but boundaried style and an ability to differentiate between providing appropriate care and gratifying the client's wishes. Effective utilization of the transference and countertransference within the client-therapist relationship will provide the most healing interventions.

The client's gender-identity issues should be understood by the therapist prior to initiating discussion about them. Understanding the meaning behind the client's personal appearance can help determine if and when this topic will be approached. For example, as a child, did she "defensively detach" from her mother as a way of protecting herself from further (real or perceived) rejection? Are there some cultural influences? Is the client defending herself from male advances due to past sexual abuse?

Other essential interventions may include spiritual support, monitoring of depression, offering practical relationship skills, and encouraging the client to cultivate a support system in addition to her therapy.

The duration of treatment is generally of a long-term nature, and many benefit from two to three sessions per week, depending on the level of functioning of the client. Therapists who travel frequently, who know in advance they will not be able to continue the therapeutic relationship (e.g., they plan to relocate or leave practice), or are experiencing their own personal crises should consider carefully before accepting such a client. Therapist reliability and consistency are important elements in treating the female homosexual.

Prognosis

As in treatment of any kind, success is dependent upon many factors. Some of the factors are within the client's control—such as her motivation and determination to change, her regular attendance at sessions, and her cooperation with treatment. Other important factors determining rate of success involve characteristics of the therapist. The therapist should be capable of attachment, be well differentiated, and have adequate skills and experience, or at least qualified supervision. Other considerations for prognosis include the client's age, history, personality organization, and overall level of functioning.

I have found my work with women to be a slow and arduous process. However, the work contains its own rewards. It is always a privilege to assist a client on her journey to becoming a healthier person, and I often find myself inspired by the determination of my clients.

Because the lesbian struggle is a symptom of a woman's inner pain and conflicts, attaining the capacity for healthy same-sex relationships and opposite-sex relating is a manifestation of inner healing and growth. Many lesbian women who desire change will fully realize their goals. And even those who are elsewhere on the "success continuum" will grow and change through therapy, experiencing greater self-understanding and a sense of personal wholeness.

CHAPTER 17

Change Is Possible

Stories of Ex-Homosexuals

James R. Hill

*I*t has been alleged by pro-gay activists for some decades that change for the homosexual is not possible. However, the fact is *change happens!* There are several kinds of evidence that indicate persons can change. One rough measure of the malleability of homosexuality can be seen in recent studies of sexual behavior. For example, the study *Sex in America* indicates that 9 percent of males and 4 percent of females had had one or more homosexual experiences since puberty; but only 2 percent of males and 1 percent of females had had one or more homosexual experiences within a year.[1] About 80 percent of all persons who have ever tried homosexuality have abandoned it. Another source of data about the possibility of change are the numerous reports "Once Gay, Always Gay?" published by Homosexuals Anonymous Fellowship Services, which quotes from the published works of some forty psychiatrists and psychologists to the effect that change is possible and that they have seen it and documented it. Masters and Johnson had a better than 70 percent success rate in the transformation of both behavior and orientation in their homosexual clients.[2] Some studies have reported even higher success rates. Ruth Tiffany Barnhouse, in an article in *Circuit Rider,* notes that "the frequent claim by 'gay' activists that it is impossible for homosexuals to change their orientation is categorically untrue. Such a claim accuses scores of conscientious, responsible psychiatrists and psychologists of falsifying their data."[3]

Perhaps the most exciting evidence of transformation recently is provided by Robert Spitzer. Dr. Spitzer was the prime force behind the removal of homosexuality from the *Diagnostic and Statistical Manual of Mental Disorders* of the American Psychiatric Association (APA) in 1973. He had long believed that change from homosexuality was not a real possibility. At the 1999 convention of the APA, he saw a number of ex-gay persons protesting a proposed resolution to deny reparative therapy to persons who wanted to come out of homosexuality. He spoke with some of them. After that experience, he decided to investigate the possibility of change. He devised his own survey and concluded, much to his surprise, that, indeed, good heterosexual functioning was "achieved by 67 percent of the men who had *rarely* or *never* felt any opposite-sex attraction before the change process. Nearly all the subjects said they now felt more masculine (in the case of men) or more feminine (women)."[4]

Yet another body of evidence is available from the Christian ministries, which help lead persons out of homosexuality. I know persons in my churches who have come to Christ and as a consequence have come out of alcoholism, cocaine use, substance abuse, anger, fear, promiscuity, prostitution, serial adultery, pornography, and homosexuality. Jeffrey Satinover, a medical doctor who has worked in and written much about this field points out that many groups, such as Exodus International, are able to report near 100 percent success rates for persons who are highly motivated.[5]

Following are two testimonies of change. They are but a small sample of those I reported in my book *The Reality of Change*.[6]

Jim Gentile is a United Methodist from Philadelphia who has struggled with homosexuality for many years. He is executive director of Transforming Congregations, a ministry for those seeking freedom from homosexuality.

> My life was pretty normal run-of-the-mill suburbia until age six, when my parents divorced. From then on, my world was turned upside down, and I experienced many things children should not see until much later on in life. I left my childhood home and moved to several apartments (changing schools often) before my mother remarried and purchased another home. I was able to see my father every other weekend and vacation with him for several weeks in the summer.
>
> At age eight, I found a large supply of pornography in my old bedroom in my father's house. From that point on,

I developed a hunger for fantasy and a compulsive habit of masturbation that would enslave me well into my adult years. Name calling by other kids, such names as "fag," "homo," "queer," and "pansy," only added to my confusion, and soon I began feeling so lousy about myself that I began to believe what they said. I began experiencing ambivalence toward other boys. I wanted to be like them and to be included, yet hated the way they behaved (tough and teasing). Inadequacy in sports added to my withdrawal. Silent confusion fueled my need and set me up for the sexual abuse ahead.

In the tenth grade, a classmate of mine invited me to her Bible study. I thought she was so beautiful, both inside and out, that I could not help but say yes. I intuitively knew that she had something that I did not. She had a certain calmness about her that enabled her to handle teenage crises almost effortlessly. I figured if she got that from this Bible study, I wanted it too! After all, my life was far from calm even though I had gone to church every Sunday since I was born and did all the "right things." My secret behavior forced me to live a double life, driven by sexual fantasy and guilt.

Within one week, I asked Christ, "If you are real, and this can actually happen, please forgive me for all the junk I have done, take away these sins, and come into my life. I am desperate and ready to let go of the rope I have been hanging on to for years."

The man who led the teen Bible study belonged to a small United Methodist Church that was experiencing the outpouring of the Holy Spirit. He and his wife opened their hearts and home to me, and although they knew little about homosexuality, they knew lots about love. They held me and cried with me and, yes, even admonished me over a period of several years. This was true discipleship. As I grew up in Christ, the pastor and his family also came alongside of me to continue the work God had for me to do.

Since I accepted Jesus, my life has never been the same! I have learned to forgive my parents, others, and myself. Although this process took longer than I care to admit, it has been a thorough process of healing that continues to this day. The Bible has become a living source that I am able to understand. Prayer has become vital communication, not an empty ritual that seemed to watch requests bounce off the ceiling and land on the floor. The fellowship of other Christians became a surrogate family.

I began to search for people like myself who wanted freedom from homosexuality and, to my great surprise, found Exodus International. I attended every conference I could find on this subject and experienced healing at the deepest levels as truth and love were ministered into my soul. Understanding, inner healing, and even deliverance were all a part of my journey towards wholeness. The many ministries and courageous sisters and brothers who loved me well now share in my victory.

Moving from sexual, emotional, and spiritual brokenness to a life that is abundant is no small miracle! As I look into the eyes of my beautiful wife and three sons, I realize the loving promise of God to make all things new. By his grace "all things work together for good for those who love God, who are called according to his purpose" (Rom. 8:28). With God, all things are possible. What seems to be an insurmountable, life-gripping problem to us, in his loving eyes, is just another miracle waiting to happen!

Lee Warner is a member of the First United Methodist Church of Marshalltown, Iowa. His testimony was originally printed in the Summer 1997 edition of the *U.M.O.R.E. Beacon,* a publication of the United Methodists Organized for Renewal and Evangelism in the Iowa Conference. It was reprinted in the *Transforming Congregations Newsletter* and is reprinted here by permission of the author.

Can God, and does God, transform lives? Yes! Do you remember how God transformed Saul on the road to Damascus over 2000 years ago? God still transforms lives today. God transformed my life four years ago [now eight] while living in Des Moines.

As a child, I felt as though there was a little girl inside of me wanting to get out. I was sexually abused by an older girl when I was very young. I attempted suicide in high school, after breaking up with my girlfriend of three years. I co-habitated with a thirty-year-old man, named John, after high school. While living with John, I met Tim;

he was my age. For the first time in my life I felt the love of a man.

Three months later, I admitted myself to the Cherokee Mental Institute. I could not stand lying to my family about the life I was living. I went to the institute a gay man, and hoped I would come out "straight." It did not work. I was there three months.

I met Joann, my future wife, on a blind date, and married her six months later. I told her that if she married me, I would try my best to give up the gay lifestyle. I could not. Three years into our marriage, we were blessed with a beautiful daughter. I told God, that if she was born healthy, I would give up the gay lifestyle. She was healthy, but again I broke my promise.

As our marriage progressed, I became more heavily involved with pornography and three gay affairs. Shortly after our eighteenth anniversary, I asked Joann for a divorce.

After my divorce, I moved in with Tim, my lover of twenty years. At first, everything was going well.

One day he told me that he did not have the same feelings for me as I did for him. My world fell apart, and I lost everything, my wife, daughter, home, and now my lover. I got down on my knees and asked God to help me. I told God that I had destroyed my life, and my family's. The Lord brought people into my life who helped me see that there was a way out of gay lifestyles. With much prayer, and a lot of forgiveness, Joann and I were remarried four years ago [now eight].

For me, homosexuality is best described in Romans 7:14-25. I was sold into slavery with sin as my owner. I wanted to do what was right, but I could not. The sin inside me was stronger. When I finally fell on my knees, and let the Lord have control of my life, God could work his great miracles, to transform me into a new person.

Yes, God can, and God does, transform lives. He changed me. Thanks be to God!

Notes

1. The Church's Teaching on Sexuality

1. These issues, in turn, involve a host of other questions, but this is nothing new. Any substantive moral or theological position encompasses a host of distinct though related matters. We shall see that there are subtle connections between epistemological and ecclesiological commitments in what follows.

2. It is worth pondering why this is the case. I can think of many factors causing folk to be reluctant to write and speak. First, some think the official position of The United Methodist Church to be so obviously correct that it does not need defense. Others fear that if they take up the issue, they will be dismissed as homophobic, exclusivist, bigoted, narrow, and the like. Still others, aware of the complexity of the issues raised, feel they could not do them justice short of a large-scale book. Still others are fed up with having to spend so much time on the issue when they want to devote their energies to urgent issues in mission, evangelism, and the renewal of doctrine. In this paper, I make no claim to be comprehensive. For obvious reasons of space, I leave aside crucial pastoral issues that need attention. I also assume that the official position of The United Methodist Church can be articulated and defended in a variety of ways. For instance, I say nothing in what follows about the commitment of The United Methodist Church to entire sanctification or holiness. It is surely clear that one could approach our query from that angle without too much difficulty. Again, for reasons of space, I have not gone down this avenue.

3. I have written two unpublished papers on the issue in hand: "A Brilliantly Flawed Performance: A Response to the Report of the Committee to Study Homosexuality" (paper prepared for the delegates to the 1992 General and Jurisdictional Conferences of the Southwest Texas Conference); and "The Construal and Use of Scripture in Theology and Ethics: A Response to Victor Paul Furnish" (paper prepared for the Perkins Faculty Symposium). I have also followed the debate in England and New Zealand.

4. *The Book of Discipline of The United Methodist Church* (Nashville: The United Methodist Publishing House, 1996), Par. 65 G.

5. It is a matter of serious dispute how far the Quadrilateral can be considered constitutive of United Methodist doctrine. My own judgment is that it represents a plausible but inadequate vision of Wesley's views on authority, and it is even more inadequate as a normative exercise in the epistemology of theology.

At best, it is a piece of temporary epistemological Midrash, endorsed but not required by the General Conference.

6. The deep reason for this stems from the central place of the appeal both to Scripture and divine revelation in the Articles of Religion and the Confession of Faith. It is extraordinary how little attention is given to these documents even though they constitute the primary doctrine of The United Methodist Church and are protected by the First Restrictive Rule.

7. I use the term "canonical" here in its original sense of "listed," that is, those commitments and rulings officially adopted and listed by The United Methodist Church.

8. This may initially appear to take us away, rather than toward, the doctrine of the Church. However, one crucial factor in ecclesiology is how far churches actually commit themselves on issues of epistemology. Since the Reformation, enormous energy has been expended to make epistemological proposals canonical and binding. Contrary to recent orthodoxy on this issue, both the Anglican Church and the churches that have emerged out of Methodism have been very circumspect on this issue, so we need to proceed with caution at this point.

9. It is extremely difficult to find consensus on how to describe the various positions. My favored designation is that of "conservatives" over against "revisionists." By "conservatives," I mean those who want to conserve the present and long-standing position of the Methodist tradition; by "revisionists," I mean no more and no less than those who want to revise the present position. However, those who want to change the present teaching of the Church find the label "revisionist" tendentious and even odious. Because of this I have avoided the term, using the terms "conservative" and "liberal" to get around the problem. Frankly this is a verbal matter that should not be allowed to obscure the substantial issues at stake. There are, of course, many who want to eschew any party label; and there are some who think or hope that some way can yet be found to find a position acceptable to both conservatives and liberals. In some instances, folk in this latter group call themselves "centrists." I find this geometrical analogy of limited help in sorting through the issues. Certainly no one to date has come up with a third way that would satisfy everybody.

10. Nothing I say below should be taken as a disparaging of the appeal to Scripture. My concern, in fact, is to ensure that the appeal to Scripture not be trivialized.

11. In the same letter, Outler claims to have written (together with Harold Bosley) the pertinent paragraph cited above in the *Book of Discipline*. Parts of it were revised at the General Conference, at which it was adopted.

12. One of the fascinating features of that report was its complete failure to recognize, much less address, the ecclesiological issues at stake in the discussion. This should not surprise the perceptive reader; for, despite avowals to the contrary, the report is a brilliant tour de force as a political document. I have drawn attention to the political dimensions of the report in this paper, as cited above in note 2.

13. This will be a hard saying for many conservatives to acknowledge. Yet conservatives lose nothing of substance by coming to terms with it. In some

ways the popularity of the Quadrilateral among conservatives stems from their instinctive conviction that there is more to doing theology than simply quoting Scripture. Moreover, even those who insist on an exclusivist appeal to Scripture have relatively loose standards when it comes to actually deriving a conclusion from Scripture, so that much of the dispute at this point is entirely verbal.

14. It is clear that Wesley did this in the case of homosexual persons, as is brought out in his attitude toward the very interesting case of a prisoner named Blair at Oxford in 1732–33. Blair was found guilty of sodomy. Yet, without for one moment relaxing his commitment to the standard Christian conception of sexual morality and marriage, Wesley regularly visited Blair, got him a lawyer, aided him in the paying of his fines, and helped him deal with the persecution he received at the hands of other prisoners. Not even the adverse publicity that arose in Oxford against the Methodists on this score deterred Wesley. The details on this can be found in V. H. H. Green, "Religion in the Colleges," in *The History of the University of Oxford,* vol. 5, *The Eighteenth Century,* ed. T. H. Ashton (Oxford: Clarendon Press, 1986), 449-50.

15. Indeed, to reduce the argument to Scripture is to ignore the internal epistemic suggestions of scripture, where it appeals, for instance, to the role of conscience in moral discernment. So Scripture itself bears witness to the possibility of extrabiblical grounding for our moral claims.

16. Otherwise, the passion and tenacity tend to be explained by citing the intellectual bad faith or intellectual vice of the persons with whom one disagrees.

17. In the case of the etiology of homosexuality, there is no agreement on the scientific data. Attempts to insist on a genetic origin have been popular in more liberal circles, but these are a serious stretch from the available data. Even if genetic origin were established, this would not resolve the anthropological and moral issues at stake.

18. One of the deep failings of liberal and radical Protestants is the inability to understand this dimension of divine revelation. In part, this explains their incomprehension of evangelicals and conservatives and the tendency to reach for merely political analyses of their theology. To be sure, there are political considerations to be identified and evaluated. However, these are only part of the story.

19. For example, Mark 10:2-9, together with parallels and other relevant texts in the synoptic tradition.

20. It is perhaps to avoid addressing this text that folk prefer to speak of same-sex unions rather than same-sex marriages. But this is a mere verbal dispute. This and other texts that deal with our Lord's teaching on sexuality clearly address the issues at stake. The attempt to reduce it all to the texts that mention of the term "homosexual" is simply evasive. One has only to make the same move on rape or incest or sex with children to see how ludicrous this linguistic reductionism is.

21. This is extremely relevant to the pastoral situation we face with regard to homosexual practice. In the end, the aim of pastoral work, here as elsewhere, is not to get uptight about our own convictions and impose them on

others. The aim is for all of us to come to terms with the Lord and Savior of the Church. Ultimately the problem is not dealing with the *Book of Discipline,* but dealing with our Lord and his teaching.

22. One way to end the debate once and for all would be to claim that the human, finite mind is incapable of receiving or interpreting any divine revelation. This gets us nowhere, for it simply bespeaks a thoroughly incompetent deity. No robust theist can take this radically agnostic claim seriously. It is hard to believe that the God of the Jewish and Christian tradition has botched things so badly in creation and redemption that he cannot get through to us.

23. Note that I am not deploying some sort of kernel/husk distinction here. What is at issue is simply whether we possess divine revelation on the matter of marriage.

24. Frankly, we have to reckon here with the old bogey of fundamentalism and the enduring inability of many United Methodist leaders to come to terms with the internal dynamics of evangelicalism both within and without its borders. For a refreshing and stimulating recent analysis of evangelicalism, see Gary Dorrien, *The Remaking of Evangelical Theology* (Louisville: Westminster John Knox Press, 1998). Particular attention should be given to what Dorrien has to say about the emergence of postconservative evangelicalism.

25. The underlying conception of canon and norm, upon which I am drawing, has been worked out in my *Canon and Criterion in Christian Theology: From the Fathers to Feminism* (Oxford: Clarendon Press, 1998). For the particulars of the situation within United Methodism see my *Waking from Doctrinal Amnesia: The Healing of Doctrine in The United Methodist Church* (Nashville: Abingdon Press, 1995).

26. Note the subtlety at this point of the article on Scripture in Article IV of the Confession of Faith: "We believe the Holy Bible, Old and New Testaments, reveals the Word of God so far as it is necessary for our salvation. It is to be received through the Holy Spirit as the true rule and guide for faith and practice. Whatever is not revealed in or established by the Holy Scriptures is not to be made an article of faith nor is it to be taught as essential to salvation." [*Book of Discipline,* Par. 62] What is not sufficiently recognized on all sides is that a community may well insist on some material teaching, whether moral or otherwise, as binding without having to agree precisely on how it reaches that conclusion. Different folk will develop different sorts of arguments to the same conclusion even though they may agree on the fundamental warrants to be deployed. Moreover, different folk can reach the same material conclusion without sharing agreement on the warrants to be invoked. It is precisely because of this that controversial matters have to be worked through in conversation, dialogue, committee, and eventually in formal conference. This may seem to be a messy way to get things done, but it was the long-standing practice of the patristic tradition, and it is crucial for the self-understanding of connectionalism within United Methodism.

27. Consider Article XIII—Of the Church—of the Articles of Religion: "The visible church of Christ is a congregation of faithful men in which the pure Word of God is preached, and the Sacraments duly administered according to Christ's ordinance, in all those things that of necessity are requisite to the same."

Compare Article V—The Church—of Confessions of Faith: "We believe the Christian Church is the community of all true believers under the Lordship of Christ. We believe it is one, holy, apostolic and catholic. It is the redemptive fellowship in which the Word of God is preached by men divinely called, and the sacraments are duly administered according to Christ's own appointment. Under the discipline of the Holy Spirit the Church exists for the maintenance of worship, the edification of believers and the redemption of the world."

28. Reformed ecclesiology, through its discussion of the power of the keys, has made much of the issue of discipline in its account of the marks of the church. Following the Anglican tradition, we have been reticent in this domain. Thus, we have been very reserved about setting the bar too high for membership of the church, and we have placed confessional commitments at the level of clergy. It may well be that confusion in this domain has been the cause of extensive dissonance in our midst. We need an extended conversation in and around this issue.

29. There is an interesting asymmetry between conservatives and liberals at this point. Should they lose the debate and the vote at General Conference, conservatives would almost certainly leave The United Methodist Church. Liberals generally stay and come back to fight another day. What is at stake are deep convictions about the very nature of the church. This asymmetry needs a lot more analysis than I can supply here.

2. The Church—The Vow—The Witness

1. James Rutland Wood, *Where the Spirit Leads: The Evolving Views of United Methodists on Homosexuality* (Nashville: Abingdon Press, 2000), 27.

2. *The Book of Discipline of The United Methodist Church* (Nashville: The United Methodist Publishing House, 2000), Par. 161G.

3. Ibid., Par. 165C.

4. Adam Hamilton, Confronting the Controversies: A Christian Looks at the Tough Issues (Nashville: Abingdon Press, 2001), 126.

3. Ecclesial Disobedience or Ecclesial Subordination to Liberal Institutions?

1. Didier Eribon, *Michel Foucault,* trans. Betsy Wing (Cambridge, Mass.: Harvard University Press, 1991), 53. Also see James Miller, *The Passion of Michel Foucault* (New York: Simon & Schuster, 1993), 58.

2. Marx, *Capital,* vol. 1 (New York: International Publishers, 1967), 176.

3. See Adam Smith, *Wealth of Nations* (New York: Modern Library, 1965), 754. For a fuller discussion on this point, see my book, *The Divine Economy: Theology and the Market* (New York: Routledge, 2000), 190-91.

4. Jeremy Bentham, Letter XIII, "Defence of Usury," in *Jeremy Bentham's Economic Writings* (London: Blackfriars, 1952), 1:163.

5. Friedrich Hayek, *The Road to Serfdom* (Chicago: University of Chicago Press, 1994), 65.

6. Ibid., xv.

7. Smith, *Wealth of Nations,* 737.

8. Ibid., 737-38.

9. J. S. Mill, *On Liberty* (New York: W. W. Norton & Co., 1975), 97.

10. Ibid., 92.

11. John Courtney Murray, *We Hold These Truths: Catholic Reflections on the American Proposition* (Kansas City, Mo.: Sheed and Ward, 1960), 98.

12. Michael Baxter, "Writing History in a World Without Ends," *Pro Ecclesia* 5, no. 4 (1996): 445.

13. James Madison, "Memorial Against Religious Assessments," in *Church and State in the Modern Age: A Documentary History,* ed. J. F. Maclear (New York: Oxford University Press, 1995), 60.

14. See *Lemon vs. Kurtzman* (Extracts) in ibid., 472.

15. Ibid., 473. Emphasis added.

16. Tex Sample and Amy E. DeLong, eds., *The Loyal Opposition: Struggling with the Church on Homosexuality* (Nashville: Abingdon Press, 2000), 125.

17. Ibid., 156.

18. D. Stephen Long, *Living the Discipline: United Methodist Theological Reflections on War, Civilization, and Holiness* (Grand Rapids, Mich.: Wm. B. Eerdmans, 1992).

19. http://umns.umc.org/01/feb/074.htm.

20. Gerhard Lohfink, *Does God Need the Church? Toward a Theology of the People of God,* trans. Linda M. Maloney (Collegeville, Minn.: Liturgical Press, 1999), 105.

21. There are stronger theological arguments that deserve our careful consideration, which do not replace the Church's sacred teachings with the American proposition. See, for instance, Eugene Rogers's *Sexuality and the Christian Body: Their Way into the Triune God* (Malden, Mass.: Blackwell, 1999). See also Bernd Wannetwatsch's helpful review, "Old Docetism—New Morality," *Modern Theology* 16, no. 3. I do not have space to develop these arguments in this essay. I do however develop them in *The Goodness of God: Theology, Church, and the Social Order* (Grand Rapids, Mich.: Brazos Press, 2001).

4. Can "Ecclesiastical Disobedience" Serve the Unity of the Church?

1. Tex Sample and Amy E. DeLong, *The Loyal Opposition: Struggling with the Church on Homosexuality* (Nashville: Abingdon Press, 2000).

2. Jean Bethke Elshtain's warning in *Who Are We? Critical Reflections and Hopeful Possibilities* (Grand Rapids, Mich.: W. B. Eerdmans, 2000) applies to many of the essays in *The Loyal Opposition:* "I have long worried that, from time to time, those who embrace the powerful term *prophetic* for their work use it as a kind of ideological cover. 'Prophetic' too often seems to amount to denunciatory rhetoric attached to a specific political agenda. In such cases the hard scholarly work is shirked."

3. See the titles of chapters 3, 11, and 12 in *Loyal Opposition.*

4. See "Introduction," and chapters 4, 7, and 11 in *Loyal Opposition.*

5. Sample and DeLong, *Loyal Opposition,* 16, 19.

6. Ibid., 16.

7. Ibid., 157. I am not making the claim that Luther and Wesley never acted in "unjust" ways that led others to disagree with them; I am criticizing Castuera's romantic claim that the "real church" is always the progressive wave of conscientious objectors to unjust laws.

8. Eugene F. Rogers Jr., *Sexuality and the Christian Body: Their Way into the Triune God* (Oxford: Blackwell Publishers, 1999), 32.

9. I do not exempt conservatives from this critique. They, too, often couch their arguments more in terms of the culture war or concerns of the political Right.

10. Geoffrey Wainwright, "From Pluralism towards Catholicity? The United Methodist Church after the General Conference of 1988," *Asbury Theological Journal* 44 (1989): 17.

11. J. A. DiNoia, "Authority, Public Dissent and the Nature of Theological Thinking," *The Thomist* 52 (1988): 189.

12. One of the purposes of the coalition of centrists, traditionalists, and evangelicals that identified itself as "The Confessing Movement Within The United Methodist Church" was to repudiate an idolatrous attachment to the principle of "inclusivism." Note the "confession" and "repudiation" of Article III of its Confessional Statement: "We *confess,* in accordance with Holy Scripture and with the Holy Spirit's help, that Jesus Christ is the one and only Lord of creation and history. In the midst of many competing voices, the Church seeks to hear, trust, and obey Jesus the Lord and his commandments (1 Cor. 8:5, 6). True authority in the Church derives from and furthers obedience to this Lord. True authority in the Church holds the community accountable to this Lord, especially when teachings and practices arise that undermine or deny his Lordship. We *repudiate* teachings and practices that *misuse* principles of inclusiveness and tolerance to distort the doctrine and discipline of the Church."

13. Alan J. Torrance, "Towards Inclusive Ministry: The Logical Impossibility of Religious and Theological Inclusivism, Pluralism, and Relativism," in *The Call to Serve: Biblical and Theological Perspectives on Ministry in Honour of Bishop Penny Jamieson,* ed. Douglas A. Campbell (Sheffield Academic Press, 1996): 256-68.

14. Torrance's basic argument is that "*all* approaches to the truth claims and status of religions and theologies are *exclusive* of contrary positions and are in essence, therefore, 'exclusive' positions. That is they make truth claims. . . . [Therefore] the Christian faith should be interpreted from within an 'exclusivist' viewpoint (as are all religions and theories of religion) but that it is also internally *inclusive* vis-à-vis persons precisely because it is also internally *exclusive of claims* incompatible with the affirmation of the One who is of decisive significance" (pp. 259, 268). Torrance's analysis depends, in large part, on Gavin D'Costa in "The Impossibility of a Pluralist View of Religions," an unpublished paper presented to the Conference on Religious Pluralism,

sponsored by the Center for Philosophical Studies, King's College London, London, February 25, 1995.

15. Torrance, "Toward Inclusive Ministry," 261.

16. Ibid., 268.

17. Ibid., 267.

18. I am not opposed to "dialogue," having participated in both of the official dialogues sponsored by the General Commission on Church Unity and Interreligious Concerns prior to the last General Conference. Yet the overpowering mind-set of these dialogues and the local dialogues that continue to flow out of them is an inclusivist and pluralist framework that finds it almost impossible to confront the possibility of some truth-claims excluding others.

19. I would exempt the theologian William Abraham from this judgment, since his attempt to reopen questions about the so-called Wesleyan Quadrilateral has been a serious epistemological challenge to various theologies within United Methodism which appeal to the Quadrilateral for their autonomous theological visions.

20. Rogers, *Sexuality and the Christian Body*, 2.

21. Ibid., Part I: "Orientation in the Debates: Sexuality and the People of God," 15-85.

22. Ibid., 26.

23. Ibid., 35. See pp. 28-36 for the chapter "Toward An Ethics of Controversy."

24. Ibid., 37.

25. Rowan D. Williams, "Knowing Myself in Christ," in *The Way Forward? Christian Voices on Homosexuality and the Church*, ed. Timothy Bradshaw (London: Hodder & Stoughton, 1997), 13; also quoted in Rogers, *Sexuality and the Christian Body*, 85. Of course, one could remind Williams that it is difficult for many in the church not to arrive at the assumption he criticizes because they have been confronted by so many revisionists who have quite clearly endorsed wholesale doctrinal or ethical relativism.

26. Rogers, *Sexuality and the Christian Body*, 1.

5. The Biblical Witness Concerning Homosexuality

1. This essay is excerpted and adapted from the chapter "Homosexuality" in *The Moral Vision of the New Testament: Community, Cross, New Creation: A Contemporary Introduction to New Testament Ethics*, by Richard B. Hays (San Francisco: HarperSanFrancisco, 1996), 379-406. That chapter, in turn, represents a revision and expansion of Richard B. Hays "Awaiting the Redemption of Our Bodies: The Witness of Scripture Concerning Homosexuality," *Sojourners* 20 (July 1991): 17-21. (A revised version of that essay has appeared in an anthology: Jeffrey S. Siker, ed. *Homosexuality and the Church* [Louisville: Westminster John Knox Press, 1994].) Portions of the exegetical work on Romans 1 are also adapted from Richard B. Hays, "Relations Natural and Unnatural: A Response to John Boswell's Exegesis of Romans 1," *Journal of Religious Ethics* 14, no. 1 (1986): 184-215.

2. According to Jude 7, "Sodom and Gomorrah and the surrounding cities,

which, in the same manner as they, indulged in sexual immorality and went after other flesh, serve as an example by undergoing a punishment of eternal fire." The phrase "went after other flesh" *(apelthousai opisō sarkos heteras)* refers to their pursuit of nonhuman (i.e., angelic) "flesh." The expression *sarkos heteras* means "flesh of another kind"; thus, it is impossible to construe this passage as a condemnation of homosexual desire, which entails precisely the pursuit of flesh of the *same* kind.

3. Daniel Boyarin has argued convincingly that these Levitical prohibitions were understood in later rabbinic tradition to pertain only to male homosexual intercourse, in which anal penetration occurs. Other forms of male same-sex erotic activity would have been understood in this interpretive tradition as forms of masturbation, which was still frowned upon but subject to much less severe sanctions. Boyarin, noting that the Leviticus passages prohibit a specific act but say nothing about sexual "orientation," contends that the rabbis had no category corresponding to the modern idea of "homosexuality." (See Daniel Boyarin, "Are There Any Jews in 'The History of Sexuality'?" *Journal of the History of Sexuality* 5 [1995]: 333-55.) One recent critic contends that the Levitical laws originally condemned only the penetrated partner in such an encounter; however, in the final canonical form of the text, Leviticus 20:13 unambiguously states that "If a man lies with a male as with a woman, *both of them* have committed an abomination" (emphasis added). (See Jerome T. Walsh, "Leviticus 18:22 and 20:13: Who Is Doing What to Whom?" *Journal of Biblical Literature* 120 (2001): 201-9.)

4. See L. William Countryman, *Dirt, Greed, and Sex: Sexual Ethics in the New Testament and Their Implications for Today* (Philadelphia: Fortress Press, 1988).

5. John Boswell, *Christianity, Social Tolerance, and Homosexuality: Gay People in Western Europe from the Beginning of the Christian Era to the Fourteenth Century* (Chicago: University of Chicago Press, 1980), 186-87, 338-53.

6. Robin Scroggs, *The New Testament and Homosexuality: Contextual Background for Contemporary Debate* (Philadelphia: Fortress Press, 1983), 106-8.

7. NRSV translates *atimazō* as "degrading." This translation seems a bit too strong; I have rendered it here and throughout this discussion as "dishonoring," which is closer to the literal sense.

8. Scroggs, *New Testament and Homosexuality,* 113-14.

9. Dale B. Martin has recently argued that Romans 1:18-32 alludes not to the universal fall of humanity, but to an ancient Jewish myth about the origins of Gentile idolatry, as narrated, for instance, in Jubilees 11. (See Dale B. Martin, "Heterosexism and Interpretation of Romans 1:18-32," *Biblical Interpretation* 3 [1995]: 332-35.) This exegetical issue is crucial for the interpretation of the passage. It is impossible to offer here a full reply to these objections, but the following points may be noted: (1) Though Paul does not explicitly cite Genesis 1-3, there is an explicit reference in Romans 1:20 to "the creation of the world" and to "the things [God] has made"; no Jewish reader

could read this language without thinking of the Genesis creation story. (2) Furthermore, the language used in Romans 1:23 explicitly echoes Genesis 1:26-28. "They exchanged the glory of the immortal God for [the *likeness (homoiōma)* of the *image (eikōn)*] of a mortal human being or of *birds* or four-footed animals or *reptiles*" (emphases added). In Genesis, humankind, made in the *image* and *likeness* of God, is given dominion over the creatures; however, in Romans 1, human beings forfeit the glory of the divine image and instead worship images of the creatures over which God had given them dominion. Thus, idolatrous worship is an ironic inversion of the creation account. (3) Martin contends that Romans 1:18-32 cannot be read as an account of the universal fallen condition of humanity because it refers only to the spiritual condition of Gentiles, not of Jews. At the first and most superficial level, this interpretation is correct, but it fails to reckon with the larger scope of Paul's argument. In Romans 1, he employs conventional Jewish polemic against Gentile immorality; but as the argument unfolds, the reader—who may have enthusiastically applauded the anti-Gentile polemic—finds himself or herself addressed by the same word of judgment; all, Jews and Gentiles alike ("whoever you are" [Rom. 2:1]), are "under the power of sin" (Rom. 3:9). Thus, the conventional attack on Gentile idolatry turns out to be also a description of the universal human condition. This claim is fundamental to the whole logic of the letter's argument.

10. For the following examples and others, see Victor Paul Furnish, *The Moral Teaching of Paul: Selected Issues*, rev. ed. (Nashville: Abingdon Press, 1985), 58-67; Scroggs, *New Testament and Homosexuality*, 59-60. For example, the Stoic-Cynic preacher Dio Chrysostom, after charging that brothel-keeping dishonors the goddess Aphrodite "whose name stands for the [natural] *(kata physin)* intercourse and union of the male and female," goes on to suggest that a society which permits such practices will soon find its uncontrolled lusts leading to the still more deplorable practice of pederasty:

> Is there any possibility that this lecherous class would refrain from dishonoring and corrupting the males, making their clear and sufficient limit that set by nature *(physis)*? Or will it not, while it satisfies its lust for women in every conceivable way, find itself grown weary of this pleasure, and then seek some other worse and more lawless form of wantonness? . . . The man whose appetite is insatiate in such things . . . will turn his assault against the male quarters, eager to befoul the youth who will very soon be magistrates and judges and generals, believing that in them he will find a pleasure difficult and hard to procure. (Dio Chrysostom, *Discourse,* 7:135, 151-52)

Likewise, Plutarch has Daphnaeus, one of the speakers in his *Dialogue on Love*, disparage "union contrary to nature with males" *(hē para physin homilia pros arrēnas)*, as contrasted to "the love between men and women," which is characterized as "natural" *(tē physei)*. A few sentences later, Daphnaeus complains that those who "consort with males" willingly are guilty of "weakness and effeminacy," because, "contrary to nature" *(para physin)*, they "allow themselves in Plato's words 'to be covered and mounted like cattle'" (*Dialogue on Love*, 751C, E). Plutarch's reference to Plato demonstrates the point that Paul did not originate the application of the *kata physin/para physin* dichotomy to heterosexual and homosexual behavior. Its common appearance in the writings of the Hellenistic moral philosophers is testimony to a convention that can be traced back at least as far as Plato (*Laws*, I.636C), almost invariably in contexts where a negative judgment is pronounced on the morality or propriety of the "unnatural" homosexual relations.

11. Josephus, *Ap.*, 2.199, Loeb translation corrected; the allusion, of course, is to Leviticus 20:13 (cf. Lev. 18:22, 29). Elsewhere in the same work, Josephus deplores "intercourse with males" as *para physin* and accuses the Greeks of inventing stories about homosexual behavior among the gods as "an excuse for the monstrous and unnatural *(para physin)* pleasures in which they themselves indulged" (*Ap.*, 2.273, 275). Paul's contemporary Philo uses similar language in a long passage branding pederasty as "an unnatural pleasure *(tēn para physin hēdonēn)*" (*Spec. Leg.*, 3.37-42). Philo's distaste for homosexuality receives its most elaborate expression in his retelling of the Sodom story (*De Abr.*, 133-41); he charges that the inhabitants of Sodom "threw off from their necks the law of nature *(ton tēs physeōs nomon)* and applied themselves to deep drinking of strong liquor and dainty feeding and forbidden forms of intercourse. Not only in their mad lust for women did they violate the marriages of their neighbors, but also men mounted males." After a lurid description of the homosexual practices of the people of Sodom, he leads into the conclusion of the tale with an account of God's judgment of the matter: "But God, moved by pity for mankind whose Savior and Lover He was, gave increase in the greatest possible degree to the unions which men and women naturally *(kata physin)* make for begetting children, but abominated and extinguished this unnatural and forbidden intercourse, and those who lusted for such He cast forth and chastised with punishments."

12. This point is overlooked by Calvin Porter ("Romans 1:18-22: Its Role in the Developing Argument," *New Testament Studies* 40 [1994]), who defends the remarkable thesis that "Paul opposes and argues against Rom 1.18-32 throughout Romans" (p. 221).

13. For a discussion of these three images, see Hays, *Moral Vision*, 193-205.

14. John J. McNeill, *Freedom, Glorious Freedom: The Spiritual Journey to the Fullness of Life for Gays, Lesbians, and Everybody Else* (Boston: Beacon Press, 1995), 132-39. Compare the argument of Sjef van Tilborg (*Imaginative Love in John*, Biblical Interpretation Series, vol. 2 [Leiden: E. J. Brill, 1993]) that the portrayal of Jesus' relationship to the Beloved Disciple in the Fourth Gospel is modeled on the pattern of same-sex love relationships in Hellenistic antiquity.

15. Luke Timothy Johnson, *Decision Making in the Church: A Biblical Model* (Philadelphia: Fortress Press, 1983), 95-97; and Jeffrey S. Siker, "How to Decide? Homosexual Christians, the Bible, and Gentile Inclusion," *Theology Today* 51, no. 2 [July 1994]: 219-34.

16. See the hermeneutical guidelines proposed in Hays, *Moral Vision*, 291-312.

6. The Classic Christian Exegesis on Romans 1:22-28

1. This study presents selections largely taken from the *Ancient Christian Commenary on Scripture on Romans*, formally cited as: *Romans*, ed. Gerald Bray, vol. 6, *Ancient Christian Commentary on Scripture*, ed. Thomas C. Oden (Downers Grove, Ill.: InterVarsity Press, 1998), hereafter cited as *ACCS NT* 6.

I am deeply indebted to Gerald Bray for this superb translation of much previously inaccessible patristic material on Romans.

2. Augustine, *The Spirit and the Letter*, 19.12, in *Library of Christian Classics*, 26 vols., ed. J. Baillie et al. (Philadelphia: Westminster Press, 1953–66), 8:209.

3. Gennadius of Constantinople, *Pauluskommentare aus der griechischen Kirche: Aus Katenenhandschriften gesammelt und herausgegeben* [Pauline Commentary from the Greek Church: Collected and Edited from Catena Writings], ed. K. Staab (Munster in Westfalen: Aschendorff, 1933); hereafter *NTA*.

4. Presumably by free volition.

5. Ambrosiaster, *Corpus Scriptorum Ecclesiasticorum Latinorum* [Commentary on Paul's Epistles], 90+ vols. (Vienna: Hoelder-Pichler-Tempsky, 1866–), 81:41, 43; hereafter *CSEL*.

6. Pelagius, *Pelagius's Commentary on St. Paul's Epistle to the Romans*, trans. Theodore de Bruyn (Oxford: Clarendon Press, 1993), 67; hereafter *PCR*. *ACCS NT* 6:49.

7. Augustine, *Augustine on Romans: Propositions from the Epistle to the Romans, Unfinished Commentary on the Epistle to the Romans*, ed. Paul Fredriksen Landes (Chico, Calif.: Scholars Press, 1982), 3; hereafter *AOR*. *ACCS NT* 6:41.

8. Augustine, *On Nature and Grace*, in *Fathers of the Church: A New Translation* 100+ vols. (Washington, D.C.: Catholic University of America Press, 1947), 86:39; hereafter *FC*. *ACCS NT* 6:41.

9. Chrysostom, *Homilies on Romans 3*, in *A Select Library of the Nicene and Post-Nicene Fathers of the Christian Church*, 14 vols., ed. Philip Schaff et al. (Buffalo, N.Y.: Christian Literature, 1887–94; Grand Rapids, Mich.: W. B. Eerdmans, 1989–94), 11:352-53; hereafter *NPNF. ACCS NT* 6:43.

10. Theodoret, *Interpretation of the Letter to the Romans*, in *Patrologia Graeca*, 166 vols., ed. Jacques-Paul Migne (Paris: Migne, 1857–86), 82:64; hereafter *PG. ACCS NT* 6:45.

11. Romans 1:24 RSV.

12. Chrysostom, *Homilies on Romans 3*, in *NPNF* 11:354; *ACCS NT* 6:44.

13. Origen, *Commentarii in Epistulam ad Romanos* [Commentary on the Epistle to the Romans], 5 vols., ed. T. Heither (Freiburg im Breisgau: Herder, 1990–95), 1:144; hereafter *CER. ACCS NT* 6:43.

14. Pseudo-Constantius, *The Holy Letter of St. Paul to the Romans*, in *Ein neuer Paulustext und Kommentar* [A New Pauline Text and Commentary], 2 vols., vols. 7 and 8 of *Vetus Latina* (Freiburg im Breisgau: Herder, 1974), 2:25-26; hereafter *ENPK. ACCS NT* 6:44.

15. Augustine, *Letters* 187.29, in *FC* 30:243; *ACCS NT* 6:46.

16. Ambrosiaster, *Commentary on Paul's Epistles*, in *CSEL* 81:49; *ACCS NT* 6:44.

17. Ibid., 81:51, italics added; *ACCS NT* 6:46-47.

18. Pelagius, *PCR* 67; *ACCS NT* 6:48.

19. Chrysostom, *Homilies on Romans 4,* in *NPNF* 11:356, italics added; *ACCS NT* 6:47.

20. Ibid.; *ACCS NT* 6:47.

21. Pseudo-Constantius, *Holy Letter of St. Paul to the Romans,* in *ENPK* 2:26; *ACCS NT* 6:47.

22. Pelagius, *PCR* 67; *ACCS NT* 6:47.

23. Tertullian, *The Chaplet,* in *Ante-Nicene Fathers,* 10 vols., ed. Alexander Roberts and James Donaldson (Buffalo, N.Y.: Christian Literature Publishing Co., 1885–96; Grand Rapids, Mich.: W. B. Eerdmans, 1951–56; 1978–80), 3:96; hereafter *ANF. ACCS NT* 6:46.

24. Ambrosiaster, *Commentary on Paul's Epistles,* in *CSEL* 81:51; *ACCS NT* 6:47.

25. Cyprian, *To Donatus 9,* in *FC* 36:14-15; *ACCS NT* 6:47.

26. Ambrosiaster, *Commentary on Paul's Epistles,* in *CSEL* 81:53; *ACCS NT* 6:47.

27. Chrysostom, *Homilies on Romans 4,* in *NPNF* 11:356; *ACCS NT* 6:48.

28. Ibid., *NPNF* 11:356-57; *ACCS NT* 6:48.

29. Cyprian, *To Donatus 9,* in *FC* 36:15; *ACCS NT* 6:47.

30. Chrysostom, *Homilies on Romans 4,* in *NPNF* 11:356; *ACCS NT* 6:48.

31. Ibid., *NPNF* 11:355-56; *ACCS NT* 6:47.

32. Origen, *CER* 1:156, 158; *ACCS NT* 6:46.

33. Ambrosiaster, *Commentary on Paul's Epistles,* in *CSEL* 81:53; *ACCS NT* 6:48.

34. Ibid.; *ACCS NT* 6:49.

35. Chrysostom, *Homilies on Romans 5,* in *NPNF* 11:360; *ACCS NT* 6:49.

36. Manicheans, who viewed the flesh as such as evil.

37. Chrysostom, *Homilies on Romans 5,* in *NPNF* 11:359; *ACCS NT* 6:48.

38. Gennadius of Constantinople, *Pauline Commentary from the Greek Church,* in *NTA* 15:359; *ACCS NT* 6:49.

39. Chrysostom, *Homilies on Romans 4,* in *NPNF* 11:355. *ACCS NT* 6:47.

7. The Real Disagreement

1. 1 Timothy 2:11-12.

2. See especially Romans 16:3-16 for an accessible and extensive, if not exhaustive, list.

3. Compare the absence of homosexual leadership to such role models as Ruth, Esther, Deborah, Mary, the mother of Jesus, Mary who sat at the feet of Jesus, the first evangelist in the Samaritan woman at the well, among others. There is a multitude of examples of women who are lifted up as examples of faithfulness, obedience, and leadership and not one corresponding example of a homosexual viewed in like manner.

4. It would be unfair not to acknowledge that some contemporary scholars have offered creative interpretations redefining the expression of homosexual acts in ancient culture to overcome negative biblical references. However, a full discussion of those proposals is beyond the scope of this essay.

5. Synod of Carthage, A.D. 394.

6. Given the claim that the Bible is authoritative for issues addressed specifically, it is easy to draw the mistaken conclusion that it is likewise unscriptural and therefore inappropriate to ordain women, an issue discussed earlier in the essay. However, that conclusion does not necessarily follow. Ordination falls under the rubric of church order and administration, which is not clearly defined in the Bible and is subject to change in accordance with the ebb and flow of the needs of the church, i.e.: the current task force assessing change to the structure of UM administration. Moreover, gender is amoral; that is, the capacity for new life in Jesus Christ, as well as transformation and sanctification, is unrelated to gender, although closely related to sexuality. Sexual immorality in either gender is seen to be a serious obstacle to growth in the life of Christ for the individual, while gender is irrelevant to the process. Finally, as mentioned earlier, there are biblical precedents for women in leadership in both the Old and New Testaments, but there is no comparable evidence of or role model for gay or lesbian spiritual leadership anywhere in the Bible.

7. Certainly, recent years have witnessed an impressive and exciting resurgence of scholarship not only defending the rationality of belief in God but also the belief in God's self-disclosure; however, while gaining respectability, that scholarship remains somewhat marginalized and inaccessible in the academy.

8. Article V, Par. 103, p. 60. "The Holy Scripture containeth all things necessary to salvation; so that whatsoever is not read therein, nor may be proved thereby, is not to be required of any man that it should be believed as an article of faith, or be thought requisite or necessary to salvation."

9. The Rev. Keefe Cropper observed that, while raising his sons, he did not teach them to lie; the ability occurred spontaneously during their childhood. Lying came very naturally to them, an observation almost universally experienced by other parents as well.

10. Tom Griffith, "Give a Cheer for Our Evangelical Brothers and Sisters," *Open Hands*, (Winter 1995): 14.

8. The Creation/Covenant Design for Marriage and Sexuality

1. John Stott, *Same-Sex Partnerships? A Christian Perspective* (Grand Rapids, Mich.: Baker Book House, 1998), 36.

2. Thomas E. Schmidt, *Straight & Narrow? Compassion & Clarity in the Homosexuality Debate* (Downers Grove, Ill.: InterVarsity Press, 1995), 47.

3. From Michael Swift, "For the Homoerotic Order," *Gay Community News* (15 February 1987). Quoted in Marshall Kirk and Hunter Madsden, *After the Ball: How America Will Conquer Its Fear and Hatred of Gays in the 90s* (New York: Plume Books, 1989), 361.

4. Kirk and Madsden, *After the Ball,* 361-66.

5. Schmidt, *Straight & Narrow,* 50.

6. Ibid.

7. Stott, *Same-Sex Partnerships,* 71.

8. David Seamands, *Good News* (January-February 1992), 16.

9. Contentious Conversations

1. *The Book of Discipline of The United Methodist Church* (Nashville: The United Methodist Publishing House, 1988), Par. 304.3; 304.6f; 332.6.

2. John Leo, "Is There an Echo?" *US News & World Report* (July 23, 2001).

3. Tom W. Smith, "Adult Sexual Behavior in 1989: Number of Partners, Frequency of Intercourse and Risk of AIDS." *Family Planning Perspectives* 23, no. 3 (May/June 1991): 102.

4. Sally B. Geis, "The Human Faces of Homosexuality," in *Caught in the Crossfire: Helping Christians Debate Homosexuality*, ed. Sally B. Geis and Donald E. Messer (Nashville: Abingdon Press, 1994), 33-34.

5. It is beyond the scope of this chapter to discuss the nature of sin and whether committed sins are the cause or the evidence of human sinfulness. See Richard B. Hays, *The Moral Vision of the New Testament: Community, Cross, New Creation: A Contemporary Introduction to New Testament Ethics* (San Francisco: HarperSanFrancisco, 1996), 383-87.

6. See *Journal of Homosexuality* 20, nos. 1-2 (1990).

7. Description in paragraph 71 of the 1988 *Book of Discipline.*

10. Homosexuality in the Postmodern World

1. Guralnik, D. B., ed., *Webster's New World Dictionary* (Englewood Cliffs, N.J.: Prentice-Hall, 1971), s.v. homosexuality.

2. Neil Whitehead and Briar Whitehead, *My Genes Made Me Do It! A Scientific Look at Sexual Orientation* (Lafayette, La.: Huntington House Publishers, 1999).

3. For a discussion of the changes in psychiatric/psychological attitudes toward homosexuality in the twentieth century, read H. Newton Malony, "Changes in Attitudes Toward Homosexuality Among Mental Health Professionals: What Pastoral Counselors Need to Know," *American Journal of Pastoral Counseling* 3, nos. 3-4 (2001): 23-36. Further, see the Division 44 of the APA report "Guidelines for Psychotherapy with Lesbian, Gay, and Bisexual Clients" in *American Psychologist* (2001): 1440-51.

4. H. Richard Niebuhr, *Christ and Culture* (New York: Harper & Bros., 1956).

5. The most recent publications asserting the biblical support for disapproval of homosexual practice are *The Bible and Homosexual Practice: Texts and Hermeneutics* by Robert Gagnon (Nashville: Abingdon Press, 2001), and *Homosexuality: Contemporary Claims Examined in Light of the Bible and Other Ancient Literature and Law* by James B. De Young (Grand Rapids, Mich.: Kregel Publications, 2000). Both are well researched and erudite.

6. This distinction between erotic and other types of relationships can be seen in Leviticus 18, in which types of relationships other than husband and wife are eschewed. Although a number of chapters in this section of Leviticus are concerned with ritual behavior, dietary laws, and clothing, the eighteenth chapter clearly states that its teachings pertain to daily life. These rules are to be followed in order that the Israelites may not live as those around them, that

is, the Canaanites. The term "uncovering" appears again and again. It is the biblical synonym for nakedness and for relating intimately with other persons. Homosexual relationships are proscribed. In fact, they are called an abomination. There is little doubt that this was the teaching of the Hebrews for long before and after the life of Jesus. It has been the teaching in the Christian tradition to the present day.

7. Whitehead and Whitehead, *My Genes Made Me Do It*.

8. Ibid., 24-25.

9. For helpful surveys of this process, read Jack and Judy Balswick's article "Sexual Diversity: An Issue for Counselors and Pastors" in *The American Journal of Pastoral Counselors* 3, nos. 3-4 (2001): 1-21; as well as Joretta L. Marshall's article "Pastoral Counseling and Sexual Identity Formation: Lesbian, Gay, Bisexual, and Transgendered" in the same issue (pp. 101-12).

10. Jeffrey Satinover, *Homosexuality and the Politics of Truth* (Grand Rapids, Mich.: Baker Book House, 1996), 20.

11. H. Newton Malony, *Perspectives on Homosexuality: The Transforming Point of View* (Pasadena, Calif.: Integration Press, 1998), 7.

12. A recent semipopular survey of these findings can be found in Melissa Healy's article in the *Los Angeles Times*, May 21, 2001, pp. S1,6 entitled "Pieces of the Puzzle."

13. Scott Sleek, "Resolution Raises Concerns About Conversion Therapy," *The Monitor of the American Psychological Association* (October 1997): 15.

14. Malony, *Perspectives on Homosexuality*, 7-8. Joe Dallas, a changed gay person, makes this point in "Another Opinion: Christianity and Ego-Dystonic Homosexuality," in *Homosexuality in the Church: Both Sides of the Debate*, by Jeffrey S. Siker (Louisville, Ky.: Westminster John Knox Press, 1994), 137-44. Dallas suggests that many ego-dystonic homosexuals come to church seeking help but are rejected and isolated. It is no puzzle, Dallas concludes, why they become accommodated to the homosexual community where they are warmly accepted. An alternative to rejection can be seen in my article "A Practical Theology of Welcoming" (*American Journal of Pastoral Counseling* 4, no. 3 [2001]: 145-52), in which I propose a model similar to Wesley's class meetings wherein any Christian dealing with areas of life that are not in accord with God's will can find support, encouragement, and transformation.

15. Details of this study can be read at the Internet address http://www. narth.com/docs/spitzer2.html. The format of the study was a forty-five-minute telephone interview using prescribed questions. The complete data is available for use by other researchers. About one-third of the interviewees gave permission for their tapes to be made available to the public.

16. *The Book of Discipline of The United Methodist Church* (Nashville: The United Methodist Publishing House, 1996), Par. 65 G, p. 89.

17. Ibid., Par. 304.3, p. 172, emphasis added.

18. Satinover, *Homosexuality and the Politics*, 67.

19. Ibid.

20. W. F. Owen Jr., "Sexually Transmitted Diseases and Traumatic Problems in Homosexual Men," *Annals of Internal Medicine* 92 (1980): 805.

21. J. E. Allen, "Health Agenda Focuses Attention on Gay's Needs," *The Los Angeles Times,* 30 April 2001, sec. S, pp. 1, 5.

22. Malony, *Perspectives on Homosexuality,* 37.

23. Allen, "Health Agenda."

24. Joseph Nicolosi, *Reparative Therapy of Male Homosexuality: A New Clinical Approach* (Northvale, N.J.: Jason Aronson, 1991), 111.

11. Marriage

1. W. B. Wilcox, "For the Sake of the Children?" (Manuscript draft prepared June 2000 for the Public Role of Mainline Protestantism project. Robert Wuthnow, principal investigator.).

2. *The Book of Discipline of The United Methodist Church* (Nashville: The United Methodist Publishing House, 2000), Par. 331.1 I.

3. *The Book of Discipline of The United Methodist Church* (Nashville: The United Methodist Publishing House, 1996), Par. 65 G.

4. See *The United Methodist Book of Worship* (Nashville: The United Methodist Publishing House, 1992), 115-38; and *Book of Discipline,* Par. 65 C.

5. *Book of Worship,* 116.

6. Ibid., 129.

7. Paul K. Jewett, *Man as Male and Female: A Study in Sexual Relationships from a Theological Point of View* (Grand Rapids, Mich.: W. B. Eerdmans, 1975), 20, 149.

8. Joseph L. Allen, *Love & Conflict: A Covenantal Model of Christian Ethics* (Lanham, Md.: University Press of America, 1995).

9. See Jewett, *Man as Male and Female,* 58-61; Don S. Browning, Bonnie J. Miller-McLemore, Pamela D. Couture, K. Brynoll Lyon, and Robert M. Franklin, *From Culture Wars to Common Ground: Religion and the American Family Debate* (Louisville, Ky.: Westminster John Knox Press, 1997); and Allen, *Love and Conflict.*

10. Don Browning, "What Is Marriage? An Exploration" (Paper presented at the Institute for American Values Marriage Consultation, New York [25 January 2000]).

11. Derrick Sherwin Bailey, *The Mystery of Love and Marriage: A Study in the Theology of Sexual Relation* (New York: Harper & Row, 1952), 99.

12. Horace Bushnell, *Christian Nurture* (Cleveland, Ohio: Pilgrim Press, 1994).

13. Bailey, *Mystery of Love,* 105. See also Allen, *Love and Conflict;* Jewett, *Man as Male and Female;* and Browning, et al., *From Culture Wars.*

14. Jewett, *Man as Male and Female,* 148.

15. Richard A. Hunt, "Marriage as Dramatizing Theology," *Journal of Pastoral Care* 41, no. 2 (June 1987): 119-31.

16. B. W. Coe, *John Wesley and Marriage* (London: Associated University Press, 1996).

17. Allen, *Love and Conflict,* 223.

18. Ibid., 222.

19. Ibid., 226, 228.

20. Ibid., 43.

21. James B. Nelson. *Body Theology* (Louisville, Ky.: Westminster John Knox Press, 1992), 26, 91.

22. For a more extensive presentation of reasons that the roots of homosexuality are in arrested childhood development, see Charles W. Socarides, "Homosexuality Is Not Just an Alternative Lifestyle," in *Male and Female: Christian Approaches to Sexuality,* ed. Ruth Tiffany Barnhouse and Urban T. Holmes III (New York: Seabury Press, 1976), 144-56; and Louis Diamant and Richard D. McAnulty, eds., *The Psychology of Sexual Orientation, Behavior, and Identity: A Handbook* (Westport, Conn.: Greenwood Press, 1995).

23. *Encyclopedia Americana* (Danbury, Conn.: Grolier Inc. 2002), s.v. "Reynolds-Tucker Act."

24. *Book of Discipline* (2000), Par. 321, 327.

25. *Book of Discipline* (1996), 69-72.

26. Ibid., 176-77, no. 2.

27. For access to many sources across the ages, see Dana Mack and David Blankenhorn, eds., *The Book of Marriage: The Wisest Answers to the Toughest Questions* (Grand Rapids, Mich.: W. B. Eerdmans, 2001). "Justice for Marriage" by David O. Coolidge (*Family Policy* 14, no. 2 [March-April 2001]: 2-6) provides a brief overview of the civil and legal issues concerning marriage in today's political climate. Linda Waite and Maggie Gallagher (*The Case for Marriage: Why Married People Are Happier, Healthier, and Better Off Financially* [New York: Doubleday, 2000]) lift up the benefits of marriage from a secular perspective. The extensive series of books produced by the Religion, Family, and Culture project led by Don Browning provides both breadth and depth for understanding marriage today.

28. Rosemary Haughton, "Theology of Marriage," in *Male and Female: Christian Approaches to Sexuality,* ed. Ruth Tiffany Barnhouse and Urban T. Holmes III (New York: Seabury Press, 1976), 213-22.

12. Homosexuality

1. This chapter is adapted from the author's book, *Crisis in Ministry: A Wesleyan Response to the Gay Rights Movement* (Lexington, Ky.: Bristol House, 1999).

2. "Helping the Homosexual," *Leadership* 13, no. 1 (Winter 1992): 57.

13. Race and Sex in the Debate over Homosexuality in The United Methodist Church

1. For the views of The United Methodist Church on homosexuality and related issues, see *The Book of Discipline of the United Methodist Church* (Nashville: The United Methodist Publishing House, 2000), 96-101, 185, and 220.

2. For a Wesleyan understanding of sanctification, see Randy L. Maddox, *Responsible Grace: John Wesley's Practical Theology* (Nashville: Abingdon Press, 1994), 122-24.

3. *Book of Discipline,* Par. 161 G.

4. E. Brooks Holifield, *A History of Pastoral Care in America: From Salvation to Self-Realization* (Nashville: Abingdon Press, 1983), 56-66.

5. Ibid., 66.

6. Ibid.

7. Ibid., 291.

8. Ibid., 116.

14. The Incompatibility of Homosexuality and the Church

1. See John S. Mbiti, *African Religions and Philosophy,* 2nd rev. and enl. ed. (Portsmouth, N.H.: Heinemann, 1990).

16. Understanding and Treating the Lesbian Client

1. This essay was adapted from one previously published by NARTH (National Association for Research and Therapy of Homosexuality) in Encino, California and is reprinted by permission.

17. Change Is Possible

1. Robert Michael, John H. Gagnon, Edward O. Laumaim, and Gina Kolata, *Sex in America: A Definitive Survey* (New York: Warner Books, 1994), 174-76.

2. William H. Masters and Virginia E. Johnson, *Homosexuality in Perspective* (Little, Brown & Co., 1979), 402, 408.

3. Ruth Tiffany Barnhouse, "What Is a Christian View of Homosexuality," *Circuit Rider* (February 1984): 12.

4. Linda Ames Nicolosi, "Historic Gay Advocate Now Believes Change Is Possible," *NARTH Bulletin* 10, no. 2 (August 2001): 1, 28. See also *Time* (21 May 2001): 62.

5. Jeffrey Satinover, *Homosexuality and the Politics of Truth* (Grand Rapids, Mich.: Baker Book House, 1996).

6. James Hill, *The Reality of Change: Twelve Testimonies of People Who Have Left Homosexuality Behind* (Pasadena, Calif.: Integration Press, 2002).

Contributors

William J. Abraham, Albert Cook Outler Professor of Wesley Studies, Perkins School of Theology, Southern Methodist University, Dallas, Texas.

G. Lindsey Davis, Bishop of the North Georgia Conference of The United Methodist Church, Norcross, Georgia.

Maxie D. Dunnam, President, Asbury Theological Seminary, Wilmore, Kentucky.

Robert E. Fannin, Bishop of the North Alabama Conference of The United Methodist Church, Birmingham, Alabama.

Richard B. Hays, The George Washington Ivey Professor of New Testament, The Divinity School, Duke University, Durham, North Carolina.

James R. Hill, Pastor of the North Clairemont United Methodist Church, San Diego, California.

Richard A. Hunt, Senior Professor, Graduate School of Psychology, Fuller Theological Seminary, Pasadena, California.

Robert L. Kuyper, Pastor, Trinity United Methodist Church, Bakersfield, California.

D. Stephen Long, Assistant Professor of Systematic Theology and Co-Director of The Ethics and Values Center, Garrett-Evangelical Theological Seminary, Evanston, Illinois.

Leicester R. Longden, Associate Professor of Evangelism and Discipleship, University of Dubuque Theological School, Dubuque, Iowa.

Susan McDonald, Lay Delegate from the San Marcos United Methodist Church to the California/Pacific Annual Conference, Escondido, California.

H. Newton Malony, Senior Professor, Graduate School of Psychology, Fuller Theological Seminary, Claremont, California.

Joy Moore, Ph.D. Candidate in Practical Theology, London Bible College/University Brunel, London, England.

Elizabeth Moreau, Pastor, First United Methodist Church, La Marque, Texas.

Gladys and Gershon Mwiti, Directors, Oasis Ministries, Kenya.

Contributors

Thomas A. Oden, Professor of Theology and General Editor, *Ancient Christian Commentary on Scripture,* The School of Theology, Drew University, Madison, New Jersey.

Andria L. Signer-Small, Clinical Pastoral Counselor, 15462 Orange Street, Lake Elsinore, California.

Edward P. Wimberly, Professor or Pastoral Counseling/Care, Interdenominational Theological Center, Atlanta, Georgia.